GOD
WAS
A
STRANGER

MARGARET KIRK

AN OMF BOOK

Copyright © Overseas Missionary Fellowship
(formerly China Inland Mission)

First published 1980
This edition 1986

ISBN 9971–972–35–2

OMF BOOKS are distributed by
OMF, 404 South Church Street,
Robesonia, Pa, 19551, USA;
OMF, Belmont, The Vine,
Sevenoaks, Kent, TN13 3TZ;
OMF, PO Box 177, Kew East,
Victoria 3102, Australia,
and other OMF offices.

Published by Overseas Missionary Fellowship (IHQ) Ltd,
2 Cluny Road, Singapore 1025, Republic of Singapore.
Printed by Kyodo-Shing Loong Printing Industries Pte Ltd

Contents

Acknowledgements:

I am indebted to colleagues Eastern and Western for their fellowship in faith and work; to Joy Hewlett and Edith Judge for their encouragement and criticism of the text; to Michael Baart and Jane Gray (with her family) for their suggestions as young people; and to the compilers of *Tanya-Jawab tentang Injil (Dialogue concerning the Gospel*, published by *OMF-BPK* Jakarta), a book widely used among students.

Preface

After many years in Indonesia, I was living in New Zealand again, because frail old parents needed someone to care for them. At home one day, while sorting out the contents of some cupboards for mother I came across several old pillowslips, apparently full of letters.

"They're yours," she said. "All the ones you've ever written!"

I was aghast! I had written almost weekly for twelve years.

"If the day comes when you have time on your hands," she explained, "it might be good to set down some of those experiences."

"You mean write a book!" I smiled at mother's unlikely dreams.

"Yes, of course," she smiled back. "About all those young people — the ones I used to pray for. You know, I felt that I really knew them."

So, partly to please her, I started drafting a plan.

It was only after my parents had both died, that I

had that time on my hands my mother knew would come. I set to work again, sorted and read some of those letters, did related research, and began to clothe the skeleton draft with flesh and blood.

Chepto's story is anchored in a crisis period of modern Indonesian history when the young republic was being convulsed by a war of ideas; when the spoils of war were the hearts and minds of its citizens, and when the enemy almost succeeded in dealing a death-blow to its hard-won freedom.

Chepto's background is typical. His experiences have been and still are being shared by many students.

But Chepto himself is a fictitious person. His character is inspired by a multitude of young people, and his search for a supreme loyalty relates to the deepest longings of young people everywhere.

Getting into focus

Imagine you are able to look through the camera's eye on a spacecraft as it scans the earth hundreds of miles beneath. When its orbit passes over South East Asia, Indonesia appears like a necklace of emeralds flung across the equator. The largest green jewel, glinting like a teardrop over there in the West, is Sumatra. That big round jewel fit for a Sultan's signet ring, is Kalimantan. Next to it is Sulawesi, a rough uncut stone with an odd shape as if the lapidarist still has to finish his work on it. Halmahera, in the far North East, is another unfinished gem.

The most scintillating jewel of all lies in the centre of the group. It is a near-perfect rectangle with multiple facets shooting out green lights — the island of Java!

These large jewels are linked by tens of smaller gems like Bali, Timor and Ambon — and thousands of mere emerald chips. The jewels are spread on a deep blue, satin-textured cloth that is luminous with reflected light — the Java Sea and the Indian Ocean shimmering in the sun.

Across the eye of the spacecraft a fluffy, opaque film drifts. It obscures part of the necklace as if wrapping it in the finest, white tissue. You are looking at the monsoon rainclouds which float over the land from November to April, and, together with the tropical sun, give it its jungles and wealth of rice.

This is Indonesia — Republic of islands — like jewels in the sun.

But it's a remote view from a spacecraft! If you wish to know more about these islands you must get back to earth and the normal perspective to which earth-bound eyes are accustomed. There is life down there, seething and surging life, as the world's fifth most populous nation continues its struggle towards selfhood.

Get closer, over that gem in the centre of the necklace — Java! Move right in — right into the life! You can't help it. There are more people living in Java than on all the rest of the islands of Indonesia added together. People are the life of a nation. People and families. So it's close range focussing now, searching out a certain town, a particular family, and one of its members — a boy in his mid-teens. It is his story that you are about to read.

1 Teenager in Chimanuk

The bell clanged, and seconds later the students of Chimanuk middle school erupted noisily out of their building, streaming in all directions across the dirt quadrangle that served as their playground. Chepto moved faster than most. He was taller than most too — a strong fellow, with a spring in his stride, and crinkly, wavy hair that stood up on his forehead above a brown, often scowling face. When he got to the gate he paused, lifted his head anxiously as though listening for something, then, clutching his books under his arm, he jogged speedily towards the railway station. He had heard it — the familiar rumble of the afternoon passenger train approaching — and he just had to get to the station first. His younger brother Rahman would already be waiting there with some snacks to sell to the passengers bound for Jakarta.

Chepto dodged some bicycles and a woman with a basket on her head, weaving his way across the busy road outside the station. There was Rahman at his usual place by the station gate, peering into the crowd looking for him. As Chepto panted onto the platform, Rahman hoisted a basket of fresh-boiled corn cobs onto his own head, then helped Chepto to balance a tray of rice cakes on his. The train drew in slowly, but the two boys were already running beside it, their baskets window high, calling out their wares, long before it finally stopped. The hiss of the engine, the trundle of trolleys, and the babel of voices combined in an uproar. Hands outstretched from the carriage windows kept the boys frantically reaching and dodging to exchange food with money before the train started to move again — just as someone lifted the last corn cob from the basket on Rahman's head and tossed some rupiah notes onto the platform.

The boys upended their containers and Rahman's teeth gleamed in his brown face as he grinned triumphantly at his brother.

"Whew! You've got to be quick," he gasped, wiping his hand across a trickle of sweat that was tickling his nose. "There's not a grain left over. That's the last of our corn crop, and not a taste of it for ourselves. Oh well ..." He shrugged his shoulders, then, duty completed, surrendered his basket and takings to his senior partner and ran off to find his friends. Chepto scowled.

"It's all right for him," he muttered to himself. "He still thinks it's fun. But I don't — not any more." He picked up his load and started to walk home slowly, stuffing the notes more securely into the pocket of his shorts as he went. He left the main road and chose the longer way around the back of the town skirting the *sawah*,[1] because that way there would be fewer people about and he wanted to think. There were plenty of people at home too, most of the time, so a person had to do his thinking out in the *sawah*.

The *sawah* encircled the town. At the centre, close to the station, was the market, the mosque and the shops. Beyond the shops were the houses. Beyond the houses was the *sawah*. There the green and gold terraces of rice spread like a broad staircase towards higher land, until the teak forests of the foothills, intermingled with the patches of jungle, laid a limiting border of dark green across its path. Beyond that again, the volcanoes that had made the soil so productive rose up to meet the sky. In all the magnificent island of Java there was scarcely a view to equal it.

But Chepto's eyes were on his feet threading their way along the narrow earth bank that separated the water-logged rice fields — and his mind was on himself. He would soon be sixteen, and his third and final year at the middle school was drawing to an end. All this week their teacher had been coaching them, the senior class, for the end-of-year examination. Chepto wasn't sweating about it. He was a serious student and a confident one. He hoped to graduate well, then he wanted to continue at high school for three more years and so qualify

---

[1] *sawah* — the area of land where rice is cultivated.

for university. But education took money, and his family had little enough of that.

The high school was in the next town. If a person had relatives there he could go and stay with them. Some of his classmates would be doing this, but Chepto had no relations in that town. Commute perhaps? But he knew the family budget wouldn't stretch to that either.

He longed to do something — anything but stay in Chimanuk. There were a good many young people like him in this town, and he was aware that there must be millions more like him throughout all these islands. But why did it have to be him? Why should it be his luck not to learn anything? Stay home and stay stupid! That's what everyone said.

His lean, brown face puckered in a more-than-usual scowl, while his hair, that black, wavy mop, seemed to stand erect on his forehead and bristle with his frustrations. The trail he was following led into a grove of kapok trees and coconut palms with a cluster of houses sheltering beneath them, like an island in the middle of a green *sawah* sea. Chepto strode fiercely through the little settlement sending scavenging chickens clucking and squawking in all directions. Some small children ran for the shelter of their homes, and an old woman looked after him in shocked surprise as he passed on and out. A couple of hundred metres more following this muddy *sawah* track and he would meet up with the main road out of town again. He had walked a half circle. Home was in sight.

As he entered the shade of the porch in the front

of the house Chepto kicked off his muddy sandals. In the centre of the porch stood a small, round table on which his mother always spread a bright cloth and placed a vase of flowers. This was where the family entertained visitors, or just flopped when there was nothing that needed doing. So Chepto flopped with relief into one of the rattan chairs there and dropped the baskets and schoolbooks into another. Mid-afternoon was the hottest part of a hot Java day, and those who could, would still be enjoying their siesta.

Inside, the house was just one large room. Its windowless walls were made of matting loosely woven from strips of bamboo. The matting provided good shelter from wind and rain, but also allowed light and air to enter. On one side of the room, partitioned off, was a large bed-platform with space for a whole family to sleep, while on the other side was a table, chairs and a sofa.

As he sat cooling off Chepto could hear his mother, Ibu Tin, working in the kitchen which was a small separate building behind the house. He knew what she would be doing. She had got up from her rest and was preparing the rice snacks for tomorrow's train passengers. Later that night his two sisters, Titi and Parmi, would wrap up each portion of rice in a square of clean young banana leaf ready for steaming. Then the following day, when junior school was finished, it would be Rahman again who took the snacks to the station and waited till Chepto appeared to help sell them. This happened most days, except when there was a feast or when their mother was ill.

Chepto emptied his pockets and began to sort out the crumpled notes. No, he did *not* think selling cakes was fun! In fact, he was secretly embarrassed, feeling this occupation to be for younger boys only and possibly women. Certainly it was not for promising students about to graduate from middle school. But even when he had graduated — what then? It would be fourteen-year-old Titi's turn, then Rahman's, and then Parmi's and the two younger brothers. Chepto, being the eldest, had a duty to step aside and allow each one of his younger brothers and sisters the same opportunity as himself. To this his mind gave assent, but his heart yearned for greater things.

He stared out across the road where *becak*[2] and bicycle passed and people padded to and fro about their business. The notes lay neatly arranged on the table in front of him.

It was almost sunset, and Chepto was still sitting meditating on his lot when the hollow beat of a drum called him to attention. From the minaret of the *mosque*[3] in the market place a loudspeaker proclaimed the time for prayer. Everyone would obey that summons wherever he was. A man driving an empty *becak* pulled up on the roadside in front of the house, bowed his head sitting right

---

[2] *becak (pr. becha)* — tricycle with a seat in front of the driver, large enough for two passengers.
[3] *mosque* — Muslim place of worship. Minaret — tower or steeple on the mosque.

where he was, and started his prayers to Allah. But Chepto did not pray. He went on thinking.

"This evening perhaps father will be saying his prayers in a *becak* too."

Bapak Hamid, Chepto's father, was a railway clerk. For the likes of him times were difficult. For years inflation had been gradually distorting the economy, but when costs increased, wages remained unchanged. Hamid's monthly pay packet from the railway would now purchase only a few days' supply of rice for his family. Because of this, many afternoons he drove a *becak*. Other workers did other things. Everyone did something and so they "got by" one way or another, and the families got fed. Chepto knew nothing else, but his father remembered better times, and would sometimes talk about "the good old days" with his friends when they came of an evening to sit on the porch, swap yarns and smoke.

How immensely proud Chepto's father was of family traditions; how meticulous with all his religious observances! Two of Hamid's brothers had made the pilgrimage to Mecca and so earned the distinguished title of Haji, and one of Ibu Tin's brothers was a *kiai*[4] in Jakarta. Chepto remembered having met these uncles as a youngster. The feelings of awe and respect for them that had been instilled into him and his brothers by their parents was still very real. Naturally Bapak Hamid, re-

---

[4] *kiai* — spiritual leader at the mosque.

membering his own upbringing, made sure that his children were properly instructed in the Koran, the Muslim holy book, from a very early age. Chepto could still recite sections of it from memory for as long as three hours at a stretch.

"So what!" observed Chepto to himself from his chair on the porch. "What's the good of it anyway? What's the good of having family who have gone halfway round the world to visit the sacred city where the prophet Mohammed was born? It doesn't help me get to high school. It looks as though Allah meant us to be poor. And if that's the way it is to be, then there isn't a thing a fellow can do about it anyway." It was fate.

Out on the road, the man seated on the *becak* completed his devotions, adjusted his little black hat more securely on his head, and pedalled off. Chepto's sister Titi came in and placed a mountain of warm rice on the table in the room behind. Some vegetables in a sauce of coconut milk followed; then a dish of *sambel*, the red, hot and peppery pickle without which no Indonesian meal, however simple, is complete.

In the evening it was usual for everyone to eat when they felt like it. Hungry Chepto got up and served himself immediately. While his right hand was shovelling rice into his mouth with incredible speed, his mother came out for the money.

A faded *sarung*[5] draped Ibu Tin's figure to ankle

---

[5]*sarung* — long piece of material worn as ankle-length, wrap-around skirt.

length. Her long-sleeved blouse or *kebaya* had once been white but even now, in its discoloured, threadbare state, it still looked fresh against the contrasting darkness of her complexion. Her long hair was pulled down into a low-slung bun at the back. She looked neat but tired, and her eyes were black pools without expression. But she smiled her pleasure as she counted the notes, putting them with others in a clay pot under her end of the sleeping platform.

"Well done, Chepto," she exclaimed. "If you and Rahman keep on like this, there will be enough here for a Lebaran celebration — and perhaps a new garment for each of you." Lebaran was the holiday at the end of the yearly month of fasting during which Muslim people did not eat or drink in daylight hours. What could be more fitting than to celebrate this day with a feast, and new clothes too, if that could be managed. Thinking how hard his mother worked to fill that earthenware pot with money for family extras, Chepto began to feel just a bit ashamed of his embarrassment over selling her produce.

During the evening the older children took turns to sit under the little palm-thatched shelter by the roadside in front of the house. Here on a bench, Ibu Tin set out a small stock of kerosene in bottles, cooking oil, soap, and such cakes as remained unsold to tempt the casual passer-by. This was known as "mother's *warung*".[6] And here, by

---

[6]*warung* — roadside stall selling food or drink.

kerosene lamplight, Chepto sat peering at his school notes and studied and dreamed while awaiting customers.

2 Dead end

At the end of the year Chepto graduated. Seeing the pride and happiness in his parents' eyes brought a glow of satisfaction to him. For, whether or not a person went on to high school he was considered a man by his parents and friends when he had graduated from middle school. But what now for this man? Stay at home? For what? He knew there were no jobs in Chimanuk.

That evening, instead of just vegetables to flavour their rice meal, Ibu Tin and Titi worked long in the kitchen cutting up little cubes of meat. Rahman carved skewers out of the stiff centre vein of a palm leaf and threaded a few cubes onto each one. And Parmi, squatting on the floor, fanned charcoal embers for all she was worth! The result was barbecue fit for the occasion — saté[1] served with peanut sauce. Afterwards, when they were all

----

[1] saté — popular meat dish cooked barbecue style.

sitting in the porch laughing and bantering, father said:

"Chepto, I am giving our *sawah* over to you to work it. I will advise, of course, and we will all help, but you will be responsible."

"I would like to help too, if we can put fish in it," burst in Rahman. It was a common practice to breed fish in the *sawah* during the growing period while the fields were flooded.

"Frogs would be less bother," suggested someone else.

"I think we will let the school children carry on selling at the station," continued father Hamid with a meaningful glance at Rahman.

Chepto heaved a sigh of relief at the prospect of release from the duties of childhood to take up the responsibilities of manhood. His father's *sawah* was small, but it would produce enough grain to feed the family for a few months, and therefore was a helpful subsidy when it came to the business of living.

So Chepto put behind him those dreams of education and joined the ranks of the largest occupational group in the country — the peasant farmers. He worked with the families whose *sawah* bordered on his father's, sharing buffalo-power for the ploughing and man-power for everything else. "*Gotong royong*" they called it, an everyday expression meaning mutual co-operation in order to do a job more effectively. Many of his workmates were enthusiastic supporters of a farmers' organization which was working for a new deal for the man on

the land. Chepto was soon accompanying them to
meetings. It was all part of being an adult. Among
them was a core of men proclaiming their hope in
the increasingly popular Communist political party. These men were very influential in the affairs of
the organization and made many promises. Their
dogmatic style was somehow out of character with
the reserved and gracious men of tradition like
Bapak Hamid. But they meant business; they
offered economic hope, and their enthusiasm was
infectious. It all helped to make a restless, part-time
farm labourer more restless.

One October day, when Chepto's first harvest
was over and he and his mates were mending
irrigation ditches in preparation for the next
planting, Broto appeared. Broto and Chepto had
graduated from middle school together, and Broto
was another who had not been able to continue his
studies. His father drove a bus and their family also
worked in a small *sawah*. But this was scarcely
enough to keep Broto busy. He liked action, and
lots of it! He didn't care that much about study. He
hailed Chepto:

"What's the news?"

From under his big straw hat Chepto replied
with a grunt.

"Huh, as usual! What about you?"

Ignoring the question Broto came up close. He
was a stocky boy with straight black hair slicked
over to one side. His eyes, rather narrow above high
cheek bones, appeared even narrower, as they
always did when he had some scheme to unload. He

spoke in a casual whisper: "How would you like to go to Jakarta,[2] eh?"

Chepto looked startled. "What are you playing at?"

"It's not a game. Look! We can't talk here when you are supposed to be part of a work team. If you're interested, see you at the *wayang*[3] Wednesday evening. It's a birthday party for Kartini, the headman's daughter, and her father is having a *wayang* show. The whole town will be there. No one is going to notice a couple of fellows talking among that mob." And Broto strolled off.

Chepto was eaten up with curiosity, for Broto was always up to something. He determined to take up his friend's invitation. Kartini had been in his graduating class also, but she had gone on to high school.

The headman's property was large and his home spacious. The special guests sat on the porch with the family, while an extension of palm-thatch roofing had been created to house the *wayang* personnel: the *dalang*[4] and his puppets, and the mini-orchestra of gongs and cymbals. Kartini was helping to greet people, dressed in *sarung* and shimmering *kebaya,* her hair plaited in a high knot and decorated with flowers. Chepto would have liked to go up and ask her how it was at high school,

---

[2]Jakarta — The capital of Indonesia.
[3]*wayang* — a cultural entertainment in the form of puppet theatre dramas depicting ancient legends.
[4]*Dalang* — puppeteer and director of the wayang.

but in less than a year his old schoolmate had become so poised and aloof that he felt like an oaf. So he just kept his distance, slouching in the shadows with a sharp eye out for Broto. Groups of people drifted in, and the soft hum of their chatter filled the grounds. An unknown number stayed near the trees, in the shadows cast by a brilliant moon, their presence only betrayed by the many glowing cigarette ends.

After a welcome speech by the host, the orchestra started to tinkle, the *dalang* launched into his squeaky nasal recitation of the ancient legend, and the wooden puppet dolls began to move across the stage under the glare from a couple of pressure lamps. Chepto knew all the wayang stories off by heart, of course. He had just stepped out into the moonlight the better to see his favourite character appear, when Broto tapped his shoulder and pulled him back into the shadows again.

"Well? Have you been thinking about Jakarta?" His voice was a tense whisper.

"Uh huh," grunted Chepto. To himself he muttered, "Get on with it. Don't be so mysterious. I'm not going to say what I think until I know what you are at." Broto began again.

"There's no future here. I don't have a job. Neither do you. I'm going to the city where others have gone: there must be lots of jobs there, and money too."

"Are you so sure? How do you know?"

"Well, the others never came back, did they?" Broto reeled off a few names of young people a year or so older, who had left Chimanuk for the capital city and not returned.

"No." Chepto didn't know what else he could say. Young people left every year and didn't come back.

"If you come to the city, your mother will have one less mouth to feed — and a big one at that! Don't you have an uncle who is a *kiai* in Jakarta?" asked Broto.

"Yes, my mother's brother. He's somewhere there, but we have never been to his place."

"Well, your parents have. That is what family is for — to be made use of." Broto always saw the possibilities.

"What about the rice harvest and the corn crop?"

"If you want to advance you have got to make a sacrifice." Broto was faintly patronizing. "Your family will manage the crops as they always have. There isn't much really. Your *sawah* is not even as big as ours. Your corn is only a patch in your back yard. For them, it will be just like when you were at middle school." He paused, and took a quick look at the wayang before the final assault. "Just think what it will mean to return with your own cash in your own pocket! Your father will be delighted because you have proved yourself able to stand on your own feet," Broto concluded persuasively.

Surely his friend was right, reasoned Chepto.

"All right. How do we get there?" he asked.

So they planned in perfect privacy, while all around them the *wayang* enthralled Kartini's birthday guests till dawn.

With the help of Broto's father who drove a minibus for a transport company, they could get relieving jobs as driver's assistant, loading, unloading, and supervising passengers and fares on a one-way Jakarta run. It sounded reasonable.

But Chepto could not tell his family the real extent of his plans. He simply said that Broto had asked him to be his companion on a visit to family in Jakarta, and that they would be staying with Broto's relatives. If Bapak Hamid suspected anything further, he said nothing. Young people learned early to be independent.

One day, when no one was about, Chepto searched among his father's papers, found the address of his uncle, the *kiai*, and copied it. His plans were then complete.

The day dawned when a mini-bus crammed with people and luggage, and with the two boys as assistants, made its way towards the capital city. Chepto and Broto had to spring out and in again at every stop. Between stops they just clung on wherever they could get a toehold. As long as they were aboard that was all that mattered! That night, lying exhausted on their sleeping mats in Broto's relatives' home, they congratulated themselves and thought how simple it had been.

Broto's uncle and family welcomed them, though their house was small and crowded. In fact, the unbelievable thing about Jakarta wasn't the wide streets and the traffic, nor the concrete high-rise buildings, nor the handsome mosques and monuments, which admittedly, they had noticed on the

way in. Rather, it was the packed-in feeling in this
suburb, where the houses had no open ground
around them as in Chimanuk. There were just
buildings and alleyways, sometimes scarcely wide
enough for two people to pass; and more buildings
and alleyways, and drains that carried storm water
and city refuse of all kinds.

Broto explained to the family that he wanted to
make his uncle's house their base till they found
work. The uncle held out his hands in a welcoming
gesture and his mouth smiled.

"As my brother's son you are welcome," he said
to his unexpected guest. But his voice was not
welcoming and his eyes conveyed nothing. "Has my
brother sent me a letter?" he enquired.

"No, uncle. He has sent his son, which is better,
isn't it?" Broto was cool.

"Very well. My sons will help you." He waved
his hand in the direction of the young men of the
household, but their manner was even less welcoming.

For two weeks Chepto and Broto tramped the
area with no results. Chepto got some free meals
when he watched a *mee*[5] seller's stand for an hour at
a stretch to relieve the owner. Jobs were not easy.

As an office worker, Broto's uncle had the usual
problems feeding his family on his salary. But here
in the city there was no *sawah*, not even a yard big
enough to grow corn. They never did find out what

---

[5]*mee* — a spaghetti-like dish to which spices, chopped-up meat and
vegetables have been added.

Broto's young cousins did. One night Amin, the eldest, declared that he lived by his wits.

"Everyone has a racket," he said. "Guerilla economy, that's what it is!" He shook his long straggly hair out of his eyes and continued with a sneer: "And if you two want to stay here, you will have to start doing the same."

The boys began to feel uneasy. They could not go on eating the food Broto's aunt struggled to provide without contributing. Politely but firmly, his uncle advised them to return home. So they moved off the following morning, too embarrassed to stay longer, but also too embarrassed to go back to Chimanuk!

Towards the end of a day of indecision hanging around the minibus terminal, they thought they spotted a familiar figure. At the back of the building, one of the drivers was peering into the innards of his vehicle. He looked to be siphoning petrol into a can. When he straightened up they saw it was Amin! He closed the bonnet of the minibus and moved off discreetly. So that was Amin's racket! He would sell on the black market when petrol stations were out of stock — which they frequently were.

That night the boys spent rolled up in their *sarungs* on a grassy bank under a bush by a canal, determined that the next day they would seek out Chepto's uncle the *kiai*.

At sunrise, after washing his face in the canal, Chepto felt in his pocket for the address. It wasn't there. He examined the money pouch at his waist and found a few *rupiahs*, but no address. Well, there wasn't anywhere else to look. A pick-pocket? Who knows. It wouldn't have been been hard, especially while they slept. Chepto's mind was numb. There were about five million people in Jakarta — and his uncle was one of them!

As usual, it didn't take Broto long to decide his next move.

"I'm going back to uncle's place," he declared. "Amin said he would show me a few things." Chepto was at a loss. What could he say?

"It's your family. You can do that if you like, but I can't," he said. "I'll go home, I suppose." But he knew his money pouch did not contain enough cash to pay his fare to Chimanuk.

After Broto went, Chepto sat in the hot morning sun and stared across the canal. On the other side was an identical grassy bank, but beyond that, instead of an open area with bushes like the one where they had slept the night, a factory wall rose. Against the wall clustered poor shelters of bamboo matting, boxes, old tins, and cloth stretched on sticks. The area between wall and canal, about four metres wide, was teeming with squatter families. Chepto knew that most of them had been lured from a peasant life in the country, by rumours of a great city's wealth and opportunity. He wondered how many would go back if they could. A puff of wind made him screw up his nostrils. The canal stank!

Chepto got up and went to find the only person he knew — the *mee* vendor. That charitable man agreed to feed him in exchange for kitchen duties and sleeping on the premises as night watch.

Chepto saw Broto again twice. The first meeting was by chance. Broto was pleased with himself, had new clothes, and had obviously found a footing in the city. Through Amin, he had become enthusiastic about the popular Communist Youth Movement.

"Our country needs this," cried Broto. "They really have ideas about how to squash inflation and get ahead — jobs for all, every farmer his own land, real equality. Our ancient class structure has had its day." And there was lots more. He pressed his friend to join the movement.

Chepto didn't have time for political meetings, but he overheard plenty of gossip from the patrons of the *mee* parlour. The vision of equal opportunity for all was good all right, but there were other, more radical attitudes that troubled him. Would these ideas fit in with his father's views? Chepto did not think so. Bapak Hamid would say that revolution was continuous, something ongoing since the day of independence from Dutch colonial rule.

"To build a nation we must all work and endure till conditions improve," he would conclude patiently. But endure for how long? And things weren't improving!

There was a tenseness about Jakarta. Public feelings, easily aroused, were likely to explode into violence. When that happened people were often not really sure what they were being violent about. There was a lot of anti-foreign talk, but Chepto had not set eyes on a foreigner since he arrived.

"Destroy imperialism!" voices cried. "Get the foreign influence out!" The pressure was on, and demonstrations by angry, marching youth were becoming more and more familiar. Chepto was confused. A buildup like this directed people's eyes away from the real struggle in which he and Broto, and their families, and millions like them were so deeply involved — the day-by-day struggle for survival with dignity.

Then Broto appeared for the second time. There was going to be a large demonstration in front of a foreign embassy. It was Chepto's privilege to participate and show his feelings for his country, persuaded Broto, until Chepto could not refuse his friend.

When the day came, Chepto emerged from the maze of shops and alleys where he lived. Along the wide main highway the demonstrators were marching with drums beating and voices raised in a rhythmic, shouted chorus. All along the route to their target their numbers kept swelling, until finally a swarming, seething mob closed in on the building. Police were there, but they simply cordonned off the area and stood by to watch events take their course. A car crept around the perimeter of the mob, but it was soon hemmed in by the mass of humanity controlling the highway.

Chepto was never sure what actually happened. Angry cries became louder. There were shouts, crashes, and the splintering of glass. The crowd surged, and Chepto with it. The little car was on its side and burst into flames. Some shots rang out, and the sea of people dissolved like a great wave receding. Only a few ringleaders were left high and dry, struggling in the arms of the police.

Chepto found himself hurrying off in the opposite direction with some fellows he recognized from the local post office. One of them confided that he was there because he had been afraid not to be. Pressure was strong in the post office.

When Chepto returned to his duties after several hours absence, the attitude of the *mee*-vendor was definitely cooling.

"Any more of these political waste-time sessions and you can go and live with your unruly friends," he declared briskly.

Chepto didn't fancy any more of them just then. The pressure of association with Broto and his colleagues was becoming uncomfortable and he knew only one way to deal with it. He was bored with dish-washing and chopping up vegetables to flavour the *mee*, and the only clothes he possessed would not last much longer. Alone that night in the premises, he decided to return home.

Before dawn he was on his way to the nearest railway station. There he bought a one-way rail ticket for as far as his cash-in-hand would allow, which was about a third of the way to Chimanuk. It got him onto the platform and into the train. The train was so crowded that no ticket inspector was ever going to have the chance to examine his ticket again. He stayed put, jammed upright in a cul-de-sac by a toilet door, and jumped off at Chimanuk.

3   Chepto takes a chance

Hoping that Bapak Hamid was not on duty at the station, Chepto slipped out onto the main street of Chimanuk. It would be easier if he were to meet his mother first. He turned his steps towards home. It was good to breath the fresh, bright air of the country after the sweaty bodies on the train. He passed through the business area around the station and came to the houses and the trees. A breeze rustled the palms. How nice it would be to climb up one of those long supple trunks again to look for a young coconut; to cut a hole in its tough outer coat, then to pour the cool liquid inside down one's throat. As he walked on towards the edge of the town, he could see beyond the fringe of coconut palms to where the water in some newly-planted patches of *sawah* glinted in the afternoon sun. This was his own place. Suddenly it had become rather special, and even held prospects for him.

There was the house. The corn growing in the

yard had been harvested and some cobs were spread on a mat to dry in the sun. Entering the porch, Chepto called out diffidently. There was a noise at the back. In a moment Ibu Tin came through from the kitchen and started to sob a welcome as she embraced him.

"Chep, we did not know where you had got to, or what had happened ... no news ... you never wrote." And Chepto found that his own cheeks were wet. The children were bursting with curiosity, but Chepto wouldn't say much.

That night Bapak Hamid received him with quiet relief and few questions. After the evening meal father and son sat on the porch. Everyone else had gone to bed. Ibu Tin served clear, sweet tea on the little table, and withdrew.

"Jakarta not what you expected, my son?" Hamid queried mildly, as if Chepto had just returned from a vacation.

"That's about it, father. Nothing but crush and confusion. At least we have some land and a bit of space here. Many country people have gone to the city. They are stuck there! They live like beggars!" Chepto recalled the sight by the canal where Broto and he had spent their last night together.

"Hm!" Hamid understood. He felt badly that he had nothing to offer his children to assist them in making a way in the world. He would never have withheld his blessing on his son's venture to Jakarta, but he was grieved that the boy had felt he must do it secretly. He felt he had lost his son's confidence just at the time they both needed it

most. The younger generation was hard to understand.

While they sat in silence Hamid puffed a
cigarette. It was tobacco that tasted of cloves, and
its sweetly-fragrant haze drifted around the porch.
At last Hamid spoke again in a matter-of-fact voice:
"A few things have happened while you have been
away. We have arranged a marriage for Titi. It is to
be with Harto."

Chepto tried not to show surprise, but his eyes
opened wide. Harto had graduated from middle
school two years ahead of him. He had stayed
around in Chimanuk, and was recognized in the
town as an able, reliable young fellow. As for Titi —
well, she was his kid sister, a school leaver, gay and
dainty, still wearing her long hair in pigtails.

Bapak Hamid continued calmly:

"Harto has a job with the railway also, and he
has been working our *sawah* ." Chepto gulped at the
mention of *sawah*. Hamid went on, apparently not
noticing: "He will build a room for them onto our
house." Silence again! More had happened than
anyone could have guessed. This would be considered a good match by both families. Chepto knew
he ought to be pleased, but he was not.

His father was still talking: "My son! Your
mother's brother, Kiai Haji Hasan, has made us an
offer to finance our eldest to study at an Islamic
school." Chepto gulped again. This was the man
whose address he had mislaid when in Jakarta. His
father smiled expectantly.

"Well, what do you say to that — you who enjoy study?"

"Father, I am not worthy. It is a great honour, but — um.." He searched for words. "I am not really very religious," he added lamely.

"A great honour it is indeed, as you say," said Bapak Hamid. "And I am glad you appreciate that part of it. But you must choose. I have always given my children the right and responsibility to make choices of their own. This is in keeping with the spirit of our country's revolution. Am I right?"

Chepto nodded. "Perhaps Rahman ..." he ventured.

"Rahman is only thirteen. By the time he is ready, my brother-in-law's generosity may have found another cause to support."

Chepto could not speak. He just sat there, overwhelmed at the suddenness of everything. Why did Uncle Hasan have to make such conditions? Muslim theology was the last thing Chepto wanted to study. Now if it had been for a university education in agriculture or science ... The minutes dragged on silently while Chepto carefully examined his feet and the sandals he had used for three months solidly in Jakarta. The rubber soles at the back under his heels had worn completely away. He hadn't even earned enough money to replace his footwear.

"So that's it then?" Hamid spoke at last, softly, his voice not betraying his feelings. "You have exercised your right."

"Yes father." After a few more moments Chepto excused himself, got up, and went out into the darkness towards the roadside. He had just shattered one of his father's most cherished hopes! Yet he longed more than ever to do something, be something, in this world.

The family did not need him any longer now, since Titi's Harto was there to work the *sawah*. Dislike for Harto rose in his soul. He was back to square one! Worse than that — he would become a burden to them without some work. As he wandered along the quiet, empty highway the *sawah* frogs croaked mockingly.

One morning, after everyone else had left for work or school, Chepto headed towards the market place. His walk was slouching and slow. With each step his sandals flicked up little clouds of the dust that lay thick at the side of the road. His mind was searching for job ideas when he passed by a group of people clustered around the door of a building. It was the Christian church, which had been in Chimanuk for as long as he could remember. He had met Jonas, the pastor, though his family had never had much to do with the small group of people who worshipped there.

But these people in front of the church were not the usual worshippers. He knew some of them. They were peering at a paper fixed to the door. He might as well see what it was all about. His feet turned around in the direction of the notice, and he went over to the entrance and read:

CANDIDATES FOR SCHOOL OF NURSING,
IMMANUEL HOSPITAL, RENGAS.
ENTRANCE EXAMINATION HELD HERE
AT ONE PM TODAY.

Was that all! With his usual scowl he ambled off slowly in the direction of the market place, again kicking up dust. But there was something compelling about that scrap of paper on the church door, and his heart began to thump as he realized its potential. No qualifications mentioned! No entrance fee! Man — why not give it a go? If you pass — you pass. If not — you fail. That's all. It's what Allah wills. What is there to lose?

Chepto pottered around the market place for the rest of the morning, then, just before one o'clock, he was back to find the church door open. Inside, a man about his father's age, with a round wrinkly face, was setting out writing gear on some tables. When he had finished Pastor Jonas motioned Chepto to a seat, and soon, several other young people entered. He recognized two who worshipped at Pastor Jonas's church. They exchanged nods.

The examination was concerned with mathematics, Indonesian language, comprehension and general knowledge. It could have been easier, but then, he had been away from school for a year and he felt he had begun to forget. It seemed that while he sucked his ballpoint others wrote on and on. When time was up the pastor dismissed them gravely with: "Come back in three weeks for results."

Chepto went off, but said nothing to the family about what he had been doing all afternoon. The days dragged by till at last he stood before the church door again.

"Ah. You are the one I have been waiting for," beamed Pastor Jonas as he opened it. "You passed your examination."

Chepto's mouth opened. "What about the others?" he asked.

"You were the only successful one, my boy."

Chepto's mouth opened wider, and stayed open. The pastor held out his hand, but Chepto did not see it.

"What about those two Christians?" Surely they were not likely to fail their own, he thought. The pastor shook his head and thrust a letter into Chepto's trembling hand.

"There was no one else," he said. "This is your appointment for an interview with the head tutor. Congratulations."

Chepto withdrew in amazement. The will of Allah, he thought.

4 Student lifestyle

Rengas — what would it be like?

In his own Chimanuk, gazing across the great stretch of *sawah* to where it merged into mountains, Chepto had often tried to picture the city he knew lay beyond.

Now, in the bus on the long climb from the coastal plain, he would soon be finding out. This time there had been nothing secret about his departure plans. All the family knew why he was going. Bapak Hamid was delighted that his son had at last found something into which his energies could be channelled, and Ibu Tin had delved into her clay pot to help purchase the basics for starting life as a student once more. Then, just as the bus was about to leave, his mother had run back into the house to get something. She came out with a packet which she carefully slipped into his hands.

Once the journey had begun he had opened one corner of the packet just enough to feel inside. He had guessed as much! It contained charms; some smaller packets covered with strange writing and a round stone wrapped in a cloth. Long ago, these articles had been purchased from a magician who had put his spell upon them. They were a source of supernatural power to their owner. They could be useful for gaining A grades in examinations, for attracting a desired girl-friend or boy-friend, or indeed for turning almost any situation to the owner's advantage.

Chepto knew that his mother's gift was costly, for these precious objects were her own, handed down through her family. She was determined that her son should have the best.

Through the bus window the scene sped past — lowlands, forests, gorges, rushing rivers, terraced hillsides, sprawling mountains. Chepto was in the heartlands of the Sundanese, his father's people. Those farming communities in the valleys would be closeknit, exclusive; the bond of family would be strong and its loyalties demanding. Like Bapak Hamid, the people would be gracious-mannered and lovers of tradition.

While Chepto continued to dwell on his ethnic origins, the bus ceased the ear-tingling roar it had been making ever since it left the plain. Its driver made a stop to refill the steaming radiator, and then drove quietly downhill towards the city.

Rengas lay before them. Famous as an educational centre, every year it welcomed thousands of young people from all over the Indonesian archipelago. Rengas was a city of students.

Chepto found the hospital at the end of a long

becak ride from the bus stop. Rekso Road, the highway past the hospital gates, extended from the heart of the city right out into the country, like a great artery pulsating with life. Chepto became part of its life stream when his *becak* joined the throng of varied vehicles travelling up and down it. Everyone was moving at his own speed, so progress was slow. It gave him time to look around. Everywhere he saw the same muted orange tiles covering little, low-roofed homes. The houses were built close, often separated by nothing more than a single-file lane. Everywhere people thronged the sidewalks and encroached on the highway, fetching and carrying, buying, bargaining and selling.

Suddenly the *becak* dodged around a pothole and almost collided with a motor scooter which, in turn, just missed skidding into a wayside fruit stall. The driver cursed, and Chepto hugged his armful of possessions and yelled, as they swerved off the road and through a gate. They jerked to a stop at the foot of a flagpole from which fluttered a red and white flag. "Immanuel Hospital" announced the notice above a building entrance. There was no mistaking it.

The architecture was old-style; long, low, single-storied buildings cunningly arranged around hidden courtyards, and all connected by covered walkways. An oasis of grass and trees filled the open ground around the buildings, and a single exit-entrance served the whole complex — the gate that opened into the hubbub of Rekso Road.

During the next few weeks students converged on

the hospital from far and near. Many preparations had been made to ensure a warm welcome for the new class. How different, Chepto thought, from the way things had been when they had turned up unexpectedly at the home of Broto's relative in Jakarta.

Even so, it was a minor shock to find himself living in a hostel with ninety other fellows. His particular dormitory housed twelve raw recruits like himself. Although he had never been in the habit of sleeping alone in a room, he was secretly glad of the degree of privacy offered by his top bunk. A fellow called Rusdi occupied the bunk beneath him. All new together, they kept the room filled with chatter and speculation about what would happen next, and shared a tingling of expectancy at the thought of becoming part of something that reached out and touched the whole community.

Students came from different islands, each with his own distinctive customs and language. Circulating around the hostel it wasn't hard to overhear snatches of unfamiliar conversation where the owners of the voices were from Sumatra, or Bali, or some other place. Chepto began to appreciate the existence of a national language — Indonesian! Like every schoolboy, he had been obliged to learn and use it from junior grades onwards, lapsing into his native Sundanese as soon as he had got out through the school door. But now, the concept of "one nation; one language", nurtured through school days, was coming alive for him. How else could he, born in West Java, enjoy friendship with colleagues who had come from other areas to study here? A newly-awakened understanding of nationhood began to surpass his childhood pride in things Sundanese. There were other islands beyond Java. They were a nation of islands. He was proud of being Indonesian.

After a few weeks of living and sharing in hostel life, Chepto discovered more differences. Some of his mates were rich, or appeared so, but the great majority were like himself — living from hand to mouth. Some were polite, some were rough and crude; some worked keenly, while others cheated regularly. About half were Muslim, there were a few Hindus from Bali, and the rest were Christians.

There were bewildering moments for newcomers, yet never a time when a person could not seek the advice or solace of Bapak Yakub, the housefather (and hospital chaplain) and his kindly wife. Their apartment, at one end of the boys' hostel, had a door that was never closed.

Bapak Yakub was a spare, upright man with close-cropped gray hair which marked him for the respect due automatically to the elderly. His eyes, partly hidden by loose folds of skin over upper eyelids, saw much more than they appeared to. He seemed to understand also that there were differences between life in a country town and life in a city hospital.

At first, regular hours really bugged Chepto after the "elastic time" of the country. In Chimanuk, for instance, a function never began until all the guests had arrived. No matter how long they took to come, no one was ever said to be late. But here at the hospital a fellow even had to be quick for meals. There were set hours, and more than once, Chepto had arrived late at the hostel dining area where the plates lay with their mountains of rice and vegetables dished ready, and found his gone!

Eating with cutlery was a chore too. At home there were techniques using thumb and fingers of the right hand — and everyone knew food tasted better eaten like that. The new life certainly was different.

It wasn't long before the recruits had met the medical director, Dr Hartono, the head tutor, and other hospital leaders. How interesting too, to meet the foreigners on the staff! Working together with their own doctors and nurses were some who had come from Western countries, including Bapak Yakub's opposite number, Ibu Anna, who was the housemother in the girls' hostel. The idiosyncracies of this group always proved a good talking point in the hostels.

The first weeks of the new life were spent in the classrooms, mastering preliminary subjects and practising basic nursing skills. Then, with some of the newness worn away, they started in the wards actually caring for sick folk. Finding one's place in a ward team, Chepto decided, was quite like the "*gotong-royong*" co-operative of the rice farmers back home. Everyone did everything, so that there were times when some jobs got done more than once and other jobs did not get done at all.

Oh well — not to worry! It was something to turn on a tap when you needed water for washing, instead of having to heave it up from a well as in most homes in Chimanuk.

Lectures continued almost daily. They always seemed to be excusing themselves from the ward and rushing away at a busy time; or, if off duty, leaving the football field halfway through a game, or being woken from the sleep of the weary — just to attend some lecture! Yet, to the hungry mind of Chepto, it was all knowledge, and, whereas the pace proved too hectic for some, he took it in his stride.

It was the day of an early afternoon lecture. Some of the dorm members who had worked mornings, had flopped onto their bunks for a quick siesta beforehand. Chepto had scarcely closed his eyes, it seemed, when he was aware of Rusdi kicking at his mattress from below and calling up to him.

"Come on Chep, time for class!" Oh no! It was the one session that bored him. Bapak Yakub led it, and it wasn't to do with nursing at all. Chepto rolled over muttering, and covered his head with a pillow till all the others had pounded out, and the room was left empty and silent. He could just imagine them. Every week at this time, Bapak Yakub stood there with his Bible open in one hand and the chalk in the other, going on and on about Allah. His eyes would narrow to mere slits, until you could swear they were closed, and he would continue his lecture as if he had memorized it. Chepto would gaze at Yakub's face, but in reality, he was gazing a little to the left of the direct line, which happened to be the neck of a girl student sitting directly in front of him — and he had worked out how she managed that coil effect with her long, sleek hair.

But what was Bapak Yakub saying? Jesus, who was the Son of God, he talked about mostly. The idea was offensive. How could Allah have a son? And they had killed him! How could Allah have allowed someone like His son, if He had one, to be shamed and defeated like that? Then there was all that about his rising from the grave. Well, of course his followers told it how they wanted it! He was just another prophet, and there were plenty of them.

It was all very irritating when you had to make out you were listening. And Bapak Yakub expected everyone to attend, just as they did the other lectures. A lot of fellows went along out of respect for the old man. Chepto had to admit he was good to have around the hostel, always available, never in a rush. And then, as this was a Christian hospital, wouldn't one expect to find what Christians believed being taught here?

So Chepto reasoned himself into a more accepting state of mind. But he continued to dislike this particular lecture hour, and after his first absence, it wasn't hard to find ways of excusing himself on other occasions.

Ramadan, the Muslim month for fasting, was approaching. It was the custom for those wishing to observe the fast to arrange with the hospital kitchen for special food supplies which they themselves would cook and eat during the night hours. And Chepto, after sitting in on Bapak Yakub's lectures at times when he could not find a reason to absent himself, was more than ready to identify with them. So, when the list came around for the names of students who wished to take part in the fasting, Chepto wrote his signature with an extra flourish.

For four weeks nothing passed his lips during daylight hours. When working and attending lectures as well, it was a hard discipline. It started as fun, with the fasters laughing and making a noise in the early hours, trying to get their food cooked and eaten and the leftovers cleaned up before daybreak. But towards the end of the month all of them were weary because of broken sleep, and very "scratchy".

Chepto stuck it out for pride's sake, but his heart remained somehow indifferent. This would do, he thought, to demonstrate his faithfulness, but any further involvement he avoided. If the extent of his grounding in the Koranic teaching, received as a boy at his father's hand, got to be known, then they might expect a much deeper allegiance from him. And this, Chepto did not care to give.

Lebaran, the day of the breaking of the fast, promised to be a truly festive holiday. Rice harvests had been good everywhere. Bapak Hamid had been able to send money to his son in Rengas to pay the bus fare home for the occasion. More homesick than he would admit, Chepto managed to arrange duties to suit, wrapped a change of clothing in a *sarung* and took off to Chimanuk.

At home, Rahman was preparing to graduate from middle school, and then to claim uncle Hasan's still-valid offer to finance his education. He was most excited about going off to Jakarta to study. Titi and Harto were married, and living in the additional room that had been built onto the house for them. Titi had not fasted because she was pregnant. Harto had not bothered to fast. Chepto, who was always quick to criticize his brother-in-law, felt his actions were disrespectful. The fact that someone under Bapak Hamid's roof, and married to his daughter, should not follow the lifestyle of the household, was nothing short of insulting! Chepto bristled with injured family pride.

He had heard as well, that Harto and some others of the younger set in Chimanuk had joined the local Communist party. If that were so, then perhaps some more pressing interests had contributed to Harto's laxity. Forgetting his own uncertain motives for maintaining the fast, Chepto challenged Harto:

"Brother, have you stopped observing our traditions?"

Harto looked surprised, but replied coolly: "No. Of course not. This one is optional, isn't it? Why? Does it bother you?"

"Yes it does," answered Chepto hotly, his dark eyes flashing. "How can you still be a Muslim if you back the Communists and forget these things?" He didn't know why he was trying to make an issue of the matter. There was no penalty for not fasting — it was a voluntary discipline. It was just that Harto annoyed him so.

"Anyone can." His brother-in-law's answer was unhesitating. "The party ideas are modern and practical. I am behind them one hundred per cent — but I shall always be a Muslim. We can use their ideas to bring ourselves up-to-date can't we? What's got into you, Chep?" Chepto glowered at him. Harto continued: "It's unpatriotic to be so critical. Aren't we all working for a better country?" He paused, as if waiting for an answer that would conclude the confrontation, but when none was forthcoming, he started up again.

"By the way Chep, how much do you earn at that hospital?"

Chepto named the student allowance, which was a pittance, and instantly knew he had been caught off guard. An expression of disbelief and scorn crossed Harto's bland face. He looked down his flat, brown nose:

"Impossible! Scarcely enough for soap and toothpaste. Even less than my miserable salary at the railway station. But the time is not far away when we shall change all these things. You will see. We are doers, not talkers!"

Chepto was reduced to silence. His face burned and he gazed at the floor. What could you say to a fellow like Harto! He had an answer for everything. And what was worse, it was true that no one else seemed to be ready to do anything about the state of the country. He envied Harto his enthusiasm, and recalling his own reasons for keeping the fast, he grudgingly admired his brother-in-law's honesty in not keeping it. If it hadn't been Harto, Chepto might have shown a more inquiring mind towards the ideas he was so eager to expound. But Chepto didn't want to be under any obligation to a fellow like his brother-in-law. He was able to choose his own way. Meanwhile, personality clashes must not be allowed to spoil the atmosphere of a family celebration.

The feasting was simple. They had killed two of Ibu Tin's chickens that had stopped laying. For weeks beforehand the household had been preparing for this day. Rahman and his two young brothers had pounded rice grains into flour. Titi and Parmi had been helping their mother make sweet little cookies in the tin oven that sat on top of the kerosene stove, and storing them in glass jars.

The Lebaran holiday meant open house. It was a day of comings and goings. Every family circle was enriched by greetings and welcomes as one household visited another throughout the town.

When it was all over, Chepto returned to the city and night duty.

5 Conflicting loyalties

Students at Immanuel hospital quite liked working nights. For one thing there was less to do, and, because there was also less supervision, they felt freer and more relaxed.

Adjusting to the altered pattern of living, Chepto conveniently slept through several of Bapak Yakub's afternoon lectures. As a result, he did not find it easy to look Bapak in the eye when they met. His voice took on an unusual gruffness if they had to converse, and he didn't stop around longer than necessary. Even so, he couldn't help liking the old man for his unfailing kindness, and for having no favourites.

The relaxed night duty atmosphere proved too much for some who were reported asleep on duty, Chepto included! As long as your patients slept why not, they reasoned. They didn't feel too troubled about it. It wasn't doing anyone any harm. But the night charge nurse was unimpressed.

Not long after that episode, Chepto's girl friend

Dewi was disciplined by Ibu Anna, the house-mother, for returning after hours to the girls' hostel. That same night, following the session with Dewi, Chepto had slipped into his dorm without discovery.

He had been careful about girls at home. Traditionally, young people didn't mix freely, and most marriages among the people in rural communities were still arranged to the mutual advantage of the families concerned. Titi and Harto had scarcely known each other beforehand, and even during their engagement period were never alone together.

But this was the city — and things were different! The girls were different too. Take Dewi. He had first noticed her on nights. She was the kind of girl a fellow couldn't help noticing. He felt drawn towards her from the start. But she had been quick to notice him too. When it was time for the midnight snack, they would have it together. Dewi told him she liked his type. Across the coffee cups her black eyes looked sideways at him. Chepto knew she was willing him to date her. And Dewi was easy. From her, Chepto learned a lot.

They both knew about what time Ibu Anna usually did her round of the hostel before retiring. Dewi would slip in just ahead. But one evening, Ibu must have been early on the round; their plans misfired and Dewi was discovered returning late.

Chepto was furious. No crabby foreigner was going to dictate to him when he should see his girl friend. He resented Ibu Anna, and despised the

nurses whom she and her assistant Kasti encouraged and trained to lead devotions in the wards for
the patients. Kasti was keen, but what else could a
patient do but hear! Patients were a captive
audience.

There were other incidents. Some of Chepto's
first enthusiasm for the life had begun to wear off,
and he was growing increasingly critical of everything about the hospital, especially the discipline.
He just wanted to get his diploma and get out as
soon as possible. That would be two more years at
least, but he was counting the months and hoping
he could stick it out. After that, he planned to join
the army medical corps. The salary there was better
than anywhere, he had heard others say, and the
prospects were good too.

One evening, Chepto and Rusdi and others were
strolling in a gang along the walkway that extended
the length of the hospital linking all the wards.
They heard voices singing, and then another voice
raised reading. They peeped through the door of
the ward they were passing, and there was Kasti
with her group of students gathered under the light
in the centre of the ward. The student finished her
reading from the Bible, and as the next song began,
some of the nurses on duty came and joined in.
Then Kasti launched into an enthusiastic explana-
tion of the verses that had just been read. Her clear,
incisive voice reached every part of the ward. As she
moved her head to look at each member of her
audience in turn, the lamp above spotlighted her
face and the faces of those clustered near her. In the

dimness, beyond the circle of light, patients lay back relaxed, and relatives staying on with those who needed extra care leaned their elbows on the beds. Nobody stirred.

The group of fellows stood in the shadowy doorway watching unseen. Alongside them, in a recess, were parked two large metal meal trolleys belonging to this and the neighbouring ward. They had been cleaned and loaded with small food containers, ready to be returned to the central kitchen in the morning. The boys eyed the trolleys, whispered among themselves, and then, just at the key moment in Kasti's talk, first one and then the other metal monster went trundling and clattering along the rough concrete surface of the walkway. They passed right under the ward windows, and within a few feet of the speaker!

Dismayed, Kasti and her friends still had enough presence of mind to stop, and when quiet was restored, finish the meeting. But the atmosphere had been shattered and the patients' attention was not to be regained. Members of the group moved around the ward talking briefly to individuals, and then went home.

Perhaps it was the success of that incident that inspired a series of disturbances. Other times when Kasti's group appeared, an unsympathetic staff member might find an urgent need to shift beds around, or, if the slide projector was being used, the electricity would suddenly switch off in the middle of the story. Kasti got used to such upsets. Nothing was said; no one knew anything; but everyone was aware that these were tactics employed by deliberate campaigners.

A new duty roster was due out any time. This meant a change-over of student power in almost every department of the hospital — a sort of general post to ensure all students a full range of practical experience during their training years.

On the day when the new listing did finally appear, everyone jostled around the notice board buzzing like bees in protest. Those near enough to read the vital news called out to others:

"Tati to casualty! Adih to men's medical! Emy to children's ward! Rusdi and Chepto to the operating room!" Chepto didn't hear any more. He was elbowing his way through the throng to study the board for himself. Well, it had to come sooner or later, and it meant removal from the distractions and temptations that were proving too much for him on the night shift. As he moved off he felt quite relieved. Lately, Dewi had been seen walking out evenings with someone else. Chepto's pride had suffered a blow. They were welcome, he thought, and spat on the grass verge of the walkway!

In the operating room, the long hours and the uncertainty of having to stand by for emergency calls was more than made up for by the excitement of being a member of the surgical team led by Dr. Daniel. However, the first day of the new change, all that Rusdi and Chepto could do after work was to flop on their bunks for a sleep.

Uncle Waji, who had been the supervisor of the operating suite for over thirty years, had a special programme for newcomers. He kept the pair of them on the move, running around, in and out, here and there, fetching and carrying, pushing and pulling trolleys, scrubbing instruments, cleaning up — there was no end to it! And they were hot in the coverup operating garb. The sweat ran down their bodies inside their gowns, and on the outside it dripped off their noses and their earlobes. Just when Chepto got his eyes focussed on the operating team, Uncle Waji would notice him and tell him to do something. And off Chepto would have to go, muttering through his mask to Rusdi as he went.

After a week, two more students entered the operating room. Then Chepto and Rusdi were able to chuckle behind those convenient masks to see Uncle Waji busily orientating the newcomers in the same fashion. Now, at last, they had earned the opportunity to watch what the operating team was doing, and even to assist. If Dr. Daniel was not concentrating too profoundly, he would explain the intricacies of the different surgical procedures that meant life and health to so many.

But not all could be helped. Some had waited too long in their villages around Rengas before making the expensive journey into the city — only to die away from home. Others were brought in after their own traditional remedies had failed. Sometimes they died too. If only they had come sooner, the doctors and nurses would try to explain to the families.

Still others lay in little, crowded houses just a few streets away, seemingly reluctant to seek the help that was so near. Then there were those who had come for help, but when faced with surgery rather than pills and injections just got "cold feet" and went home again to endure their fate.

Chepto remembered a man with a gangrenous leg, who would not consent to part with it because he could not face the thought of eternity without a limb. Some nurses explained that he could not face eternity without Jesus, whom God had sent to be his Saviour, and who would give him a new body.

Sometimes patients were dissatisfied, like the man who had the end of his nose sliced off in a knife battle. The surgical team sewed the flap back on, but the man's wife was not pleased with her husband's altered appearance, and was critical about having to pay for it just the same! Uncle Waji dealt with her lack of appreciation in coarse local language. Only staff of local origin really understood what he was saying, which was just as well, decided Chepto.

People also came to the hospital because they had no money, and heard that they would not be turned away in their need. And sometimes, people would be sent by other doctors who had given them up as hopeless.

That was how Hasanah came. Everyone knew about Hasanah. She was having a series of operations to complete a full-thickness skin graft. She had recently been married, and not long after her wedding, Hasanah was preparing a meal in her new home when the kerosene cooker exploded. As her burns healed, a horrible disfiguring scar developed over her neck and chest, replacing the soft, supple skin that had been burned with a vast area of knobbly, hard scar tissue. The scar tissue had steadily contracted, drawing Hasanah's chin down further and further onto her chest, until she could no longer close her mouth or turn her head, and her face was contorted into a perpetual grimace.

Hasanah had been to many doctors, but no one had been brave enough to tackle her problem. When Dr. Daniel saw her, his heart almost failed him too. He took an extra long time over his examination of her, and at last he said: "I will try, and with God's help we will manage something."

Chepto never forgot the first time he had to help bring her to the operating room. She lay on the trolley. She was trembling, he knew, because he could feel the trolley vibrating under his hand.

While they were waiting, Dr. Daniel came out from the scrubbing up room where he was preparing himself. His hands were lathered in soap and he talked through his mask. Hasanah could only see his eyes twinkling as he reminded her briefly of all they had explained to her and her husband during the preceding days.

When everything was ready, the team members gathered around, and the doctor introduced them, telling what each one did. Then he motioned towards the instrument nurse, a girl from a mountain town outside Rengas:

"Sister Ratih will pray for us." Ratih knew why she had been asked. Like Hasanah, she was also Sundanese, and would use the local West Java language which Hasanah understood best.

Chepto did not know what to think. But, he observed, the doctor treats people as though each one matters specially to him. He bowed his head respectfully.

"... for we ask in the name of Jesus our Saviour. Amen," concluded Ratih. Hasanah, comforted, whispered that no one had ever done that for her before, and Sister Lyn, the anaesthetist, started to put her to sleep.

So began the first operation in the step-by-step process of removing a large flap of skin from Hasanah's back just below her rib cage, and bringing it up to be grafted onto her neck.

During the following days of tedious and painful immobility for Hasanah, Ratih and friends from the operating room found time to slip over to her ward to encourage her.

"My body is ruined," she would moan. "My husband will not want me." She feared that he would divorce her if her looks could not be restored. The nurses assured her that no matter what happened God, who had helped her to this moment, would not forsake her.

Once Chepto went by and found one of the staff nurses reading the Bible to her. Hasanah had said she would like to put her trust in Jesus as her Saviour, but was afraid of what her family would do. Perhaps she did believe in her heart, but she never gave her friends in the hospital the opportunity of hearing her say so.

Hasanah spent months in hospital and made

many trips to the operating room. Finally, a transplant of living skin was growing firmly in position covering her neck and replacing the scar tissue that had been cut away. She went home with a wisp of a scarf around her head and across her chin to hide the remaining scars. But there was free movement for her neck, and the terrible skin tension once caused by the pull of so many contractions had been released, giving back the natural contours to her face. Her eyes danced for joy and she was beautiful once more. When she went, she took a Bible with her.

After that, Hasanah returned several times as an outpatient, and on her final visit brought her first-born, a little daughter, with her. But nobody ever knew how her heart was towards the Lord Jesus. She kept her secret, and the nurses who had cared for her kept hoping.

Countless others passed through the hospital to new life and hope, but none left their mark on Chepto as this young woman did. Being a member of the surgical team was quite the most interesting and satisfying work he had ever taken part in. His discontent had melted away. He didn't even mind too much when Uncle Waji was organizing everyone. He just learned to keep out of the way.

Chepto was utterly absorbed in the operating room work when an old friend entered his life again. It was in the evening after a warm, weary day. The fellows were letting off steam on the volley ball court, punching and spiking the ball and hooting with laughter, when someone called out: "Chepto

— a visitor!" He withdrew from the game reluctantly, and went to the guests' waiting room. As he entered, a familiar figure rose from a chair.

"Broto!"

"It's me!" Broto laughed. "No other."

"How good to see you," cried Chepto, looking him over. The same confident Broto, the leader of earlier adventures — the same magnetism, perhaps even more so.

"What's the news?"

"Where have you been all this time?"

The questions popped out simultaneously. They exchanged experiences until Broto exclaimed: "This room is a bit dreary. Why don't we stroll and talk and get some coffee at a *warung*." It was dusk and, as usual at that time, life was being lived on the street. A queue waited for the *saté* man as he squatted on the roadside behind his charcoal fire, sizzling rows of skewered meat cubes. A crowd pressed around a seller of home-made pills and potions as he dramatized the usefulness of his wares. Quite a bit cheaper than ours, thought Chepto as they passed. A mother chased her toddler with a bowl of rice, trying to give the evening meal to a wayward little citizen on the run. Youths giggled and guffawed in groups. People walked up and down all over the street.

In the buzz and chatter of Rekso Road Broto unfolded his business. He had found a niche in Jakarta. His leadership qualities had been recognized by the Communist Youth organization, and he had become involved in their recruitment and training programme. For this reason he was in Rengas.

"Chepto, old friend, it's people like you we need. Get with it now, and you will be in the right place to profit in the days to come when we are in power." There was to be a meeting at Prak Lane the following Thursday and Broto urged Chepto to come along.

"It's not far from the hospital. We will expect you," he said.

Chepto walked in silence. He felt flattered to have been sought after by a fellow like Broto. Broto was so committed yet, despite expanding responsibilities, he hadn't forgotten their friendship. Perhaps now was a good time to get on the bandwagon. And so Chepto promised to be present. As they strolled along, his mind went back to the evening of Kartini's birthday party two years ago. Then, as now, astute Broto had arranged to meet him in the protecting crowd where interruption was unlikely. They slipped into a *warung* for a snack before separating. Broto paid the bill, then took off in a *becak* while Chepto walked back to the hospital alone.

Thursday was a heavy day in the operating room. That afternoon, one of the staff on duty became ill, and word was brought to Chepto that he must stand by in the sick man's place. Just my luck, he groaned. While he was feverishly trying to find someone to stand in for him so that he could go to the political meeting, a call came to prepare for emergency surgery. By the time the operation was

completed and the place cleaned up, the gathering
at Prak Lane had dispersed.

6 Coup!

The tropical day starts early. At five in the morning, dawn breaks in the east.

The farmers of Java are already on their way to the *sawah*. In the Western highlands, the tea pickers have begun reaching for new leaf buds as they move between the rows of bushes on the hillsides, and the vegetable growers are marching out, hoes over shoulders, to tend their crops.

In the cities, the fresh food markets are a turmoil of action and a hotch-potch of smells. The traffic has started — the roar of bus and truck, the purr of delivery vans, the putt-putt of motor scooters, bells jingling on pony carts, wooden blocks clacking as hawkers with wagons or baskets announce their approach and call out their wares. And in homes everywhere, children are being hustled to do their chores before school starts at seven a.m.

The tropical dawn is brief. Within a few minutes of first light, the disc of the sun leaps out of the night. Glowing fingers of light, red, orange and gold, touch and transform the landmarks in an uncertain, gray landscape. Then, with a suddenness that dazzles, warmth and brilliance flood the world as a new day begins.

It was on a day like this, a certain historic October the 1st, just before the sun was due to appear, that Bapak Yakub tuned in to Radio Jakarta for the early news broadcast — and got no response! This puzzled him. But he got up and started to potter around while Ibu made the coffee. He would wait a while. It couldn't be his radio. He had been listening to it only the evening before, and the batteries were new.

Ibu Anna in the girls' hostel also sat puzzled before her non-functioning transistor. She had heard the day shift girls go off rather noisily to duty, and the sound of water splashing in bathrooms as the night shift returned in ones and twos, washed, and fell into bed. But from the hub of the nation there was still no news.

Ibu Anna became involved in the routine of hostel administration. Yes, those night nurses had left the taps in the washrooms running full flow to refill the water containers, and gone to bed without turning them off. Now, precious water was trickling out of the overflows.

The washrooms were small and square. A tiled tank of cold water filled one side of the room and the person bathing stood in the space that was left, first lathering up with soap, and then ladling water over herself. It was delightfully cooling but very wasteful. Water was scarce because the supply system was old, and the demand had outgrown it. No one thought it was possible to wash properly in any less water than she was using, so those who didn't bath in the mornings usually found empty tanks by nightfall. Ibu Anna sighed and went to turn off the taps.

As the morning progressed she forgot that she hadn't heard the news, until a messenger came circulating a note from the medical superintendent. The girl found Ibu Anna and burst out:

"Dr. Hartono has asked all the staff to assemble at ten in the School of Nursing auditorium." She was breathless with her exertions to cover the whole hospital complex with the letter. Anna studied it and ticked off her name on the accompanying list as having received the message.

"Something's happened in Jakarta," called out the messenger as she hurried away to the next name on the list. "Telephones are all out of action," was her parting shot as she disappeared round a corner and out of the hostel. Ibu Anna was left to puzzle what this sudden lack of communication could mean.

She informed the hostel population and, at ten o'clock, joined a hushed and uneasy staff as they assembled in the large hall. The medical superintendent was there talking gravely with some of the other doctors in a group apart. When the hall was filled, Dr. Hartono turned to his staff. His face was pale. His hands were clenched and, as he went to speak, he pressed them hard on the table in front as if he needed support. When he spoke it was with difficulty and his voice, usually so sharp and quick, seemed strained and far away.

"Someone has tried to seize power in Jakarta," he said. "The bodies of six of our top army generals have been found down an old well at an airfield on the city outskirts." It was uncertain who was heading the government. The country was awaiting some statement from the President. But no one was sure what had happened to the President either. In fact, no one was sure of anything. There was no communication with the capital. The telephone lines from Jakarta's central post office had been severed, and no one had heard anything from Radio Jakarta for many hours.

The people in the room stood silent and motionless like puppets awaiting the *dalang*. Noise from Rekso Road drifted in.

"You are to carry on as usual until we know what is happening," continued Doctor Hartono more firmly.

"There will be a curfew. No one is to be out of doors after sunset. If duty requires it, you are to have a police escort." The doctor's face moved as if he would cry. Instead, he signed to Bapak Yakub who prayed for God's mercy on the nation, His protection for all in the hospital and His strength to sustain each one in whatever duty might be theirs in the days to come.

Nurses and other staff moved back to their posts in shocked silence, their thoughts confused, their hearts fearful. What did it all mean? They could only guess.

Later that day, the Daniel household got the first real news in a bulletin from Radio Australia which confirmed everyone's worst fears. The dead generals were named. They had all been openly opposed to the Communist party! It was the Communists who were trying to topple the government by violence. It was they who had betrayed the nation.

Fear was waiting to paralyze in its grip any who let their imaginations wander out of control. All one could do was carry on, as Dr. Hartono had so wisely instructed, keep busy, and wait. New citizens demanded to be born; people got sick or had accidents, or died; the living had to be fed. Life at Immanuel Hospital, in the city of Rengas, and indeed the whole of the nation, continued with unusual quiet that day while coup and counter-coup rocked the capital city of Jakarta.

A long, tense twenty-four hours later, with radio communication to the nation re-established, one thing became clear. The government with the army was in command. The betrayers were exposed. A vicious and ruthless bid for control of the nation had failed.

Chepto worked on in robot-like fashion, the enormity of what had happened in far-away Jakarta only slowly taking hold of his senses. Several weeks had passed since Broto's visit. Broto — could he have known about this? Could he really have wanted a violent takeover? Chepto felt his head was spinning, for none of it made sense to him. Anyhow, where was Broto in all this, he wondered. But that question never did get answered. He never heard of his friend again.

The hostels were a hotbed of rumours fanned by the confining effects of the curfew. The fellows in Chepto's dorm tried to guess who might belong to the now unmentionable political party. There were a certain few on the staff who had not shown up again at work. Then they had heard that all over the country known party sympathizers had simply disappeared once it was clear that the coup had failed. Information, filtering through from all manner of sources, was shrouded in secrecy, distorted by fear, so that it was impossible to sort fact from fantasy.

One certainty emerged. A build-up of evidence pointed unmistakeably to the unmentionable party's involvement in the attempted takeover. Plans had been discovered, it was said, to eliminate anyone who was regarded as a threat to the regime of those who had tried to seize power. This was likely to include hospital leaders! So the hostel dwellers speculated on what might have happened if ... but it didn't bear thinking about!

One night, they were having a late session sprawled on their bunks.

"Wonder how the army is getting on combing the city for suspects?" someone asked. "Those who aren't dead or in prison will be on the run."

"Too right! Have you heard about Prak Lane?" interrupted another.

"That's near here."

"What about Prak Lane?"

The informant wore just a trace of triumph on his face at having captured the attention of the group. "They found a hoard of grenades and firearms," he replied.

"I heard that. And a lot of men have been arrested from that street too." Another added his bit.

"Go on! How will the prisons hold them all?" someone else asked, followed by grim chuckles all round.

"Under the earth's the place — as they planned for the generals!"

At the mention of Prak Lane, Chepto felt a queer tightness in his throat. The name triggered his memory. It was close by, someone had said. Then he had it! Broto had said it was close too. If Prak Lane had been searched so recently they might be at the hospital any time!

A cold sweat broke out all over him; nausea struck at his middle regions, and he hugged himself to keep control. The urge to get out and run, to disappear anywhere, gripped him. But he sat silent — and reason forced an entrance into his near-hysterical mind. Keep cool, it whispered. You didn't go to that meeting, remember? The emergency surgery prevented you. Then surely — your name cannot be linked with them.

He made an excuse to leave the gossiping group and backed into the shadows and through the door. It was only just in time. When he got outside he was sick on the grass. After that, he crept off to bed to hide his remaining tensions in the top bunk.

The eyes of the nation were now wide open to the real intent of Communist Party organizers. Reaction followed, like a rising tide that knew no restraints.

"The betrayers deserve the people's wrath," certain community leaders cried. They urged their followers to search out and kill, and do the nation a service. So kill they did, savagely, remorselessly. The terror started in Central Java, and was worst there, but from there it took its toll everywhere. "If we do not destroy them they will destroy us," was the cry.

The people's justice was the spirit of revenge run amok — a far more terrible thing than any justice administered by the army. "*Amok*" is a word from Java meaning "out of control" or "berserk", and in this manner, the people's justice swept the land, sometimes claiming the innocent as well as the guilty. In the months of retribution and death that followed, it was the same, no matter where. To be a known Communist was usually to become a dead one.

At the hospital everyone tried to function as usual — at least on the surface. But some of the students had not heard from their homes for weeks. When no one was sure who was friend and who was foe, even among their own families, it was wiser not to communicate but just to keep quiet and wait.

Chepto waited for news from Chimanuk with

fearful foreboding. He would have taken off for home at the first opportunity, but travel was almost impossible. Petrol was scarce, buses were scarcer. There were road-blocks everywhere, and people ready to bribe their way through where they could. Well, Chepto had no spare cash, so he couldn't get caught up in that sort of thing. Like all the others, he just had to carry on where he was and wait.

At last, someone from Chimanuk personally delivered a letter for him. Recognizing his father's finely-formed script he tore it open, almost ripping the contents in his haste. The family was safe, he read, and felt limp with relief. But Harto had disappeared immediately after the collapse of the coup. Some others in the town had been arrested. And what was this — he peered at the name — the mayor, the town's leading citizen, had gone. That was Kartini's father! Later, a packet containing the mayor's clothes had been returned to his wife! Chepto's backbone tingled. The whole thing was a fantasy. He read on.

Titi was in Jakarta with Rahman under the protection of uncle Hasan, who was a man known for his lack of sympathy towards the unmentionable party. In the city, his father hoped no one would get to know of her association with one of the nation's betrayers.

The letter ended, and Chepto stood and pondered the fate of his attractive sixteen-year-old sister, a widow, awaiting her first-born among strangers. He turned and stalked off, cursing Harto under his breath. If Harto had not already been dealt with, Chepto would have killed him with his own hands, just as some of his countrymen were doing in other places.

Chepto had never felt so miserable. In the hospital they were getting ready for Christmas. This meant that Ibu Anna and the girls would prepare a feast in their hostel and invite everyone! Although Chepto could raise no enthusiasm, he was glad they were carrying on as usual — so far as they could. It brought a sense of continuity into the chaos.

Out by the flagpole at the hospital entrance, some of the nurses were setting up a Christmas display. The idea had been sparked off by Dr. Daniel, who was a master at doing all sorts of things with junk that no one else wanted. Apparently useless material he would examine carefully, and his pleasant, drawly voice would pronounce judgement: "Yes thank you. I'm sure it will come in handy. It will be just what we need for fixing this or tying that."

So day by day, a lot of nothings were becoming something before the eyes of a circle of curious spectators. Chepto was one who lent a hand when they wanted volunteers to paint a Bible verse on a large board. He was glad to have something to fill in the empty off-duty hours. Time had become a burden.

As he painted, he thought of the religion of his upbringing, which was the pride and strength of his father. To be honest, it had never meant a great deal to him. He had followed along with the outward tokens, the rituals and the customs, but he secretly felt that there was no future in it for the modern generation. Now, emerging from the hurt and disillusionment of all that had happened, were faint stirrings of a strange new desire. Allah ... who was He anyway? For a Communist, He did not even exist! But Chepto had been nurtured on belief in God — distant, unknowable, yet a God to be worshipped. Bapak Hamid had seen to that. And now ...? What had Allah to do with all this confusion? Did He know what was going on? Did He care? How could worshipping Him have any reality? The more Chepto worked with his paintbrush, the more he wanted to understand what it was that Bapak Yakub really taught about Him week after week.

Bapak Yakub's Bible instruction class was an unchanging institution, and it was safe to predict that it would continue so as long as Yakub was. In his unruffled, unhurried way, the housefather led the students as before, almost as if there had never been a nation-shaking political upheaval.

"God's word is forever," he maintained flatly, his gaze sweeping the class from under hooded eyelids. "We need it. It is the only thing that makes sense. Without it, nothing else makes sense." Chepto wondered if Bapak Yakub's name had been one of those appearing on the unmentionable party's list of undesirable citizens.

After Christmas, Chepto stopped looking for excuses to evade this once-despised lecture hour, and began to attend Bapak Yakub's classes regularly. He recalled those other times he had sat behind his desk, ready to switch off when the talk started. You've heard often enough, his conscience muttered. Now listen! There is a difference! Deep in his once-closed mind, prejudice and confusion gave place to the growing certainty that the old man, his teacher, knew the way to God.

Then why couldn't he grasp it? Listening did not help. He didn't understand. Study did not help. He couldn't concentrate. He was restless and could find no ease of mind. He just was not able to come to grips with the truth he had been hearing over and over, despite himself, since coming to this place. He wanted badly to talk to someone about it, but pride held him back. Who would understand? They would think he was stupid!

One day after duty, Chepto drifted in through the door of the Yakubs' apartment. He didn't really know how to say what he wanted. An unvoiced longing was sealed up inside him. So he sat there, flipping the pages of a book and talking about anything for the sake of saying something. Bapak Yakub was as welcoming as ever, listened, but did not probe.

After a brief visit, the moody guest slouched off, hands thrust into uniform pockets, without really saying why he had come.

"He will be back," thought Bapak Yakub as he watched him go.

7 Night Visitor

The men's hostel was in darkness. The only sound came filtering across from the densely lived-in area beyond the hospital walls — the faint tinkle of gong and cymbal accompanying a nasal soloist. Someone over there was having a party and they had invited a *gamelan*. Outside, the moon lit up the courtyard, empty save for the lacy shadow cast by the net on the volley-ball court. A light showed the way along the covered walk that led to the hospital wards, and another glowed through drawn curtains in Bapak Yakub's flat. Yakub, his *sarung* draped around him, settled in his easy chair for a brief meditation before sleep. He thought he heard a knock and was about to ignore it, the sound seemed so uncertain. But, on second thoughts, he put aside his Bible, and forcing himself out of the chair, went to open the door.

Chepto stood outside. Two pairs of eyes met; the inscrutable old ones half hidden by drooping upper lids, and the wavering, questioning young ones. Thought Yakub to himself: "This fellow has been on my mind. I wonder why he has chosen such a time to come to me?" Looking at the troubled face before him he said aloud: "Come in, lad. Bapak has been expecting you."

Startled at such a welcome, Chepto stepped inside hesitantly. As they both sat down Bapak Yakub proceded to put his guest at ease with hospital chichat. Soon, Ibu Yakub appeared carrying a tray with two glasses of clear, sweet tea. She set it down and withdrew. While the two of them drank together Yakub made an opportunity for his late guest to speak his mind.

"How is it you are not enjoying your rest tonight?" he asked.

"I can't sleep," explained Chepto in a flat-sounding voice. He looked at his lap and twiddled his glass of tea. Yakub raised his eyebrows just a little.

"Something is burdening you, my son," commented his host. "Can Bapak help?"

Chepto did not need further prompting. He grasped the opportunity. Leaning towards Bapak Yakub, he blurted out in a rush: "I must find out about Allah. I want to know how to worship Him."

"As I supposed," Bapak was thinking. "This is why he comes after dark. If his friends knew, it might be embarrassing!" Gently probing his visitor's intentions further, he asked: "Isn't the worship of Allah something you learned from your family?"

"Yes. But those ways don't mean anything to me any more. I want to know how to worship Allah so ... so ..." He paused, searching for the right phrase.

"... so He will receive me." Silence. Chepto, his shock of wavy hair standing up on his forehead, fixed Bapak Yakub with an intense stare. Yakub sat there stroking a few long whiskers on his chin, and went on looking at nothing in particular. Finally, the old man spoke.

"When a person goes to the mosque to worship, he takes off his shoes at the door." Chepto nodded, and his host continued: "Then imagine this. Two nurses entered the hospital chapel to worship. One left his shoes at the door, and the other didn't. The one who took off his shoes started to pray, but it was clear that he did not pray sincerely. He was putting on a show so that people would consider him good. The other, who didn't take off his shoes, poured out his heart to God asking forgiveness for his sins. Who was truly worshipping Allah?" He looked at Chepto who answered readily, "The one who kept his shoes on, because he came honestly and humbly."

"Right. And God will not listen to a person if he has sin in his life, no matter what kind of worship he performs. So, when Jesus came, he did not make many rules about the way his followers should worship. What matters to Him is this: is our worship spiritual and real? For God is Spirit, and God wants this kind of worship from us."

Chepto sat glued to his chair.

"How can it be real?" he interrupted, his brows meeting in a puzzled frown. Bapak Yakub reached for his Bible, and continued:

"You must first of all come to Him with a pure

and honest heart. Allah is holy. We who are not holy are not fit to approach Him. His Word says, 'All your sins have cut you off from Him!'[1] That's why you don't feel right about worshipping Him. That's why you are so troubled and have no peace inside!" Chepto's eyes widened and he looked disbelieving. How could this old man know what was going on within him? But he did — he knew!

"My life's a mess," Chepto admitted.

"Can you tell me about it?" invited Bapak Yakub.

"I didn't come here because I wanted to learn nursing or help sick people," Chepto spoke fiercely. "I wanted an education. I came here because there was nothing else." Out it all flowed: the frustration of having to leave school, deceiving his parents to go to Jakarta, returning to find another in his place at home, and then a way out offered through Immanuel hospital. He confessed his indifference towards the traditions of his upbringing, his shock at discovering the real intentions of the unmentionable political party, and how, in all the confusion and bitterness, the very thing he had resented having to hear was that which held out hope.

"That's why I've come," he finished lamely. "To find out about God."

Yakub was a good listener. Although it was approaching morning, he behaved as if he could spare all night to hear about the troubles of his guest.

---

[1] Isaiah 59:2

"God knows about you," he said, and Chepto blinked with amazement. "If your life is a mess, He understands. He knows all that is in your heart." Chepto wondered why God should really bother about what was in his heart. But one thing he was certain of:

"My heart isn't honest before God — but I want it to be."

"That's why He sent his Son Jesus." Yakub spoke with conviction. Chepto's lips had often curled mockingly over the way the followers of Jesus spoke about Him. But this time he kept silent, and his host continued: "Jesus is able to cleanse the sin from our lives and bring us to God. You want to find God! Jesus said He was the way — that no one could come to God except through Him. When we trust in Him as our saviour from sin, then we are able to worship with a pure heart — and it's real!" Chepto said nothing. It certainly was real for Bapak Yakub.

"No one has ever actually seen God, but when we see the character and deeds of Jesus, we recognize Him." Chepto sat thinking about recognizing Allah — Allah the distant, Allah the unknowable — in Jesus, whom they had been studying about all year in Bapak Yakub's Bible classes. It was mind-boggling.

"You know, the name of our hospital explains it," Bapak Yakub began again. "IMMANUEL — it's one of the special titles given to Jesus when He was born. It means 'GOD WITH US!' That is who Jesus is."

Chepto's mind went back to the Christmas festival and the display that Dr. Daniel and the nurses had erected at the hospital gates. They had used a roll of old wirenetting, one end of which they hitched to the top of the flagpole. The rest curved right down and around the base of the pole. On the netting they had mounted outsize letters cut from the heavy black and yellow paper that had served as protective wrapping for X-ray films.

As he sat there Chepto could picture it. The letters made words that filled the whole scroll ... KASIH ALLAH TURBA ... the love of God came down among us. At night it glowed with makeshift floodlighting that had been rigged up by an ingenious hospital electrician, clearly read by everyone. Then underneath, on a very large piece of wood, was the Bible verse they had all helped to paint. It was in the Sundanese language, so that every passerby on Rekso Road could understand. "For God loved the world so much, that He gave His only Son, so that anyone who believes in Him shall not perish, but have eternal life."[2] That verse had got tucked away in his memory without his realizing, and now it had come back. He was beginning to understand too.

Love — that was the difference.

God loved. He was neither distant nor unknowable. In Jesus, he had come down among His people to save them.

God's servants loved. At work in the hospital he

----

[2] John 3:16

had seen it; the way they cared for the hopeless, for those who had no one, for those whom others had turned away. God was making His love known through His servants. He wasn't indifferent. Nor was He partial. His love was for everyone.

Then Chepto wanted desperately to be in on it — to be part of this tremendous truth that was filling his understanding. Believe, that's what he had to do! "Anyone who believes in Him ..." the verse said. That's me. How do I believe? God help me. Chepto bowed his spirit before God who had sent Jesus to be his Saviour because of love. And he knew that the burdens of the past were gone, his heart was clean, and his future, whatever it might be, in a loving God's keeping.

Bapak Yakub, from his chair, observed that God had spoken to his visitor while he was sitting there thinking it all through. There would be no need of further words from him that night. They finished their drinks, now quite cold, before he broke the silence: "Shall we talk to God about you before you go?" Chepto nodded. So they did; thanking Him for understanding, and for being able to believe.

"Goodnight. Come back again when you are ready — but try to find a better time." Bapak Yakub was smiling just a little. As he opened the door to show his guest out he gave his parting word: "You came to the hospital because you wanted to get away from something. But God sent you so that you would find Him."

"The old man is speaking in riddles," thought Chepto, but he was quite content to leave it at that.

Wearily he slipped across the moon-bathed courtyard. The *gamelan* orchestra had ceased and the soloist was silent. As he entered the dorm, the only sound that greeted him was the rhythmic breathing of his mates. He hoisted himself onto his bunk in the darkness and fell asleep.

8 Lukas shows the way

In the men's hostel a new senior student had been appointed. Lukas came from one of the farthest borders of Indonesia, the island of Halmahera. Although this island lacked such modern conveniences as electricity and paved roads, it was rich in copra, fish, teak and friendliness. Many generations of its people had been followers of Jesus, God's Son, and His church had deep roots there.

The parents of Lukas had dedicated their children to God, and hoped that some of them would become medical workers or pastors. Choosing nursing, Lukas left home to work in the only hospital on the island, five hours down the coast by sailing canoe. Having there demonstrated his ability in nursing, he was one of three for whom the church had made arrangements to train in Jakarta. The young people sailed together for Java and the big city — a trip that could take one month or three, depending on the whim of the waves, captain or cargo.

Jakarta at last — the city with huge white mosques, hotels, monuments, brick homes, wealth — and beggars who live and die in the streets. What a contrast to Halmahera! There were no beggars there. It was a beautiful island. But, by the time the three country young folk reached the school of nursing, its door had been closed to them. Lectures had already begun. They were too late.

What would they do, stranded islands from home with no money and no job? As he had been taught to do, Lukas prayed.

God heard him. A stranger, a student from Immanuel Hospital in Rengas, suggested they try to get into the training programme there, though classes had begun at Immanuel also. So they travelled to Rengas. Welcomed by Dr. Hartono, the far-from-home trio were grateful to learn that they could stay.

And now, Lukas was near the end of his final year, a leader who felt his responsibilities keenly. It was he who noticed how the new students were making out, tried to help those who had trouble finding their niche, and saw that the lonely and homesick were befriended. He sensed the disruptive elements too, and usually managed to deal with them at their source.

Lukas was a small, wiry, fine-featured fellow, with the deep-set eyes and the darker-than-usual skin tones that marked him as a man from the Eastern islands. There were students from Java who didn't feel happy about having someone from a place like Halmahera over them. Lukas didn't let that concern him unduly.

Small he might be, but he had great capacity, and he worked at maintaining a harmonious liaison between students and those in authority. His capacity for work was only exceeded by his capacity for friendliness. Perhaps it was the environment of his friendly home and people, the gift of his inheritance, but whatever it was, the friendliness spilled over and allowed Lukas to "get alongside" people in a way that others envied.

Some of the hostel inhabitants appreciated him as an elder brother because he had "got alongside" them when they needed a friend; others would have preferred another senior because Lukas always spoke up fearlessly against something when he felt he should; yet, whatever group they belonged to, they all respected him.

It was Bapak Yakub who mentioned fairly casually that perhaps Lukas might find time to look out for a certain fellow who had come to him for a long chat one night. Bapak Yakub's approach to anything was always delicately indirect. That was the manner of the older people. But Lukas understood his ways and got the message. So Chepto found a friend in the new senior.

Lukas was a keen footballer. The field at the back of the hospital compound knew his flying figure well. But in his spare time he would just as likely be found sprawled on his bunk reading the Bible! One day, when they were looking around for people to make a couple of teams, Chepto found him like this.

Chepto thought he might be preparing something. He knew Lukas helped Kasti's group with ward meetings when he had time, or led a group of his own.

"No, just reading," Lukas explained absently, after a polite refusal to join the sportsmen. Then with more vehemence: "What a book! Do these people ever experience life! And all the time, God's there mixed up in it with them ..." He became engrossed again, lying on his stomach, feet in the air. Chepto was impressed. What kind of a book would hold a fellow from football in his spare time!

There was so much Chepto wanted to know now, since his evening visit with Bapak Yakub. The questions kept forming in his mind even while he was on duty, until he had to tell himself firmly — get on with the job! If you don't know what you are doing about the place you can be dangerous! Then later, in the dorm, when he came to write them down, he couldn't remember them. But it didn't matter — fresh questions were there demanding an answer.

Lukas talked about spiritual matters as naturally as farmers speculated about the rice crop, or nurses gossipped over the day's happenings in the ward or casualty department. So Chepto did not find it hard to open up to him with his questions — and he began to get answers.

One afternoon, Lukas was sprawled on his bunk reading, when Chepto came along and disturbed him.

"Were you always like this — so keen on the

Bible?" he asked bluntly. The small man from the friendly island did not seem upset at the intrusion on his leisure. He leaned on his elbows and pushed his hands through his hair, thinking how best he could answer. His Bible lay open on the cover before him.

"No. I guess not!" He started to explain. It was really because of something that had happened at one of the young people's house parties organized by Ibu Anna. They had gathered in the mountains, in a once-derelict dwelling that student work-groups had slaved to redecorate as a kind of retreat house for hospital personnel. During training, most students had at least one opportunity to attend a houseparty there, but this gathering Ibu Anna had promised to arrange specially for some who were about to graduate. It had been a study retreat led by a young student for the ministry. What he had to say had so stirred them all, that Lukas and two of his mates had given themselves to serve Jesus, God's Son, with a depth and deliberateness that was new for them. " ... and somehow, this has made all the difference," Lukas confided to Chepto.

"But haven't you always believed in Him from your parents in Halmahera?" Chepto was mystified.

"Oh yes! That's just it. What I have always believed has come alive, and just means so much more for every day. I'd never have been able to tackle the appointment in the hostel before this happened. I wouldn't have known how to control my tongue for one thing. There'd have been sparks and fire every time a fellow didn't toe the line I set him — in fact, one flaming row after another." Chepto just looked! Lukas wasn't one to be offended at the way people reacted to him.

"Call it Jesus-power!" offered Lukas. "That's what it really is — His Spirit working through our personalitics helping us to be like Him. He promised He would if we let Him." With that, the senior pulled himself up to a sitting position, flipped his legs over the edge of the bunk, put his Bible on his knee where they both could see it, and invited Chepto to join him.

"God speaks to us through His Word" he said, indicating the Bible, then added thoughtfully: "I suppose that's the main reason why I enjoy reading it. And we speak to Him when we pray." Chepto nodded. He had spoken to God — in Bapak Yakub's flat! It was a moment more clearly etched on his mind than any other he had ever experienced. But he recognized that Lukas spoke to Him quite often — with a difference, as if he was having a conversation.

"Now," continued Lukas, fingering the pages of his Bible as he talked, "When you read His Word and then you come across a part of it that means something special — really hits you, so that you want to talk back to God about it — man, you've got two-way communication!" Lukas had found what he wanted in the book, and stopped turning the pages.

"Let's do it," he said. So they read and worked through an example together.

The next day, Lukas produced a small paperback. He had bought it from the mobile bookstall — a couple of display boards on wheels that found its way regularly to every corner of the hospital.

"This will help you begin for yourself," he said, handing the book to Chepto. "It's got a Bible reading and guide notes for each day." Chepto knew Lukas wasn't likely to have spare cash around when his home was all those islands away. His friend must have rationed himself on soap or postage stamps in order to make him this gift. An unusual warmth filled him as he looked down at the booklet in his hand and saw the title: PERSEKUTUAN PEMBACA ALKITAB — Scripture Union Notes — published in many different languages, the flyleaf informed him, and used by Bible lovers all over the world.

After that, Lukas began share-sessions in the hostel with whoever happened around and wanted to join in. They would each give their own thoughts about the Bible passage they had read together. Then whether a group of six or only two, they would pray concerning what had meant most to each one, asking God to help them do it. Just a sentence each — no more. But for Chepto, when he was around, it was the beginning of conversation with God.

The new senior took the Bible seriously! He would search it when he needed guidelines in dealing with situations that arose in the hostel. He would expect to find help in its pages when a student needed to be counselled. If he couldn't find what he wanted, Bapak Yakub might help, or Ibu Anna. Lukas knew there would be an answer somewhere.

In the hostel, furnishings were basic. When friends joined Lukas in one of his searches, they sprawled all over the bunks, and then, in an informal and intimate fellowship, they would thrash out current problems in the light of what they found in the Bible.

One day, Chepto and Lukas were talking as they walked along the covered way that linked the wards. When they passed under the windows of the obstetrical unit Lukas suddenly changed the subject.

"You know, Chep, you are like a new-born baby!" He nudged Chepto in the direction of lusty new-born voices, where the most recently-arrived citizens were demonstrating their wants. "Just as they need the right sort of food to grow, you too need a proper diet of spiritual food if you are to keep on growing and developing as a follower of Jesus."

Chepto burst out laughing at the unexpected advice. He couldn't help it, although he knew his friend to be serious. Lukas just smiled.

"It's an illustration from the Bible," he explained. "It really is so."

And quietly, without drama, the "new-born" started to mature. Chepto would not have said that life was different. On the outside, student life went on much as it had always done. The pace was solid. There was new knowledge to master, and new experiences daily, as they cared for sick and needy people. There were off-duty relationships and activities, and there was always sport. But HE was different! He thought about things differently.

9 Devil's toys

It was about this time that Chepto got to know Ibu
Anna. He had steered clear of the housemother at
the girls' hostel ever since his night duty nappings
and the affair with Dewi. Yet Ibu's door, like
Bapak Yakub's, always stood open. The girls, and
even some of the fellows who had come to her to
talk through their difficulties, found her ready to
listen and helpful.

She worked tirelessly at creating a homelike
atmosphere in the girls' hostel and had gradually
won the confidence of its students. This wasn't an
easy job for anyone; in addition, Ibu Anna was
from America, big, with short brown hair and blue
eyes — very foreign! She had foreign ideas too,
particularly about discipline. Chepto could remember her campaigns to get people to clean up the
toilets and to aim their banana peel in the direction
of the rubbish cans instead of just letting them stay
where they happened to fall. Her popularity rating

was low at that stage. What young person likes being told what to do by anyone, let alone by a foreigner?

When Anna arrived at the hospital, the girl's hostel had been leaderless and chaotic, and Dr. Hartono had asked her to give it her special attention. It had become an orderly, gracious place — one of the most attractive corners of the compound. It boasted painted bamboo awnings, flowers bordering each side of the path to its front entrance, and hanging fern baskets in the porch. By comparison, the boy's hostel looked quite scruffy and neglected. Most of the girls took a pride in helping to keep it nice, and enjoyed the sense of family they found there.

Whenever there was a celebration in the hostel, like Christmas or graduation, Anna delighted the girls by dressing up in the traditional *sarung* and *kebaya*. Then she would get one of them to pin a hair-piece at the nape of her neck for correct coiffure effect. The outfit was most becoming to her ample figure. Ibu Anna looked stunning, and the girls would chorus admiringly with much laughter: "A real Ibu! A real Ibu!" And, for all her foreignness, that was what Ibu Anna was.

With her large family of young adults, the housemother felt she was never quite able to relax completely. In such a diverse student body, with all members living in a confined space under the one roof, she could be sure that something was always brewing. And there were always the stirrers, finding something in the brew to make trouble about. Then others, if they weren't stirrers, couldn't mix — the seemingly incompatible personalities!

Dewi in particular had been a concern to them all for a long time. She was noisy and insolent around the hostel, and often upset her room mates by getting uptight about the smallest thing. She was quick to take offence, and on duty, no one felt they could tell her anything. She wasn't what one would call nice looking — there were more attractive girls — yet she had the hostel boys competing for her attentions. Compelling was a better way to describe Dewi's looks. And she blatantly ignored the rules!

Then she began to act strangely, just the opposite from the Dewi everyone knew. She became quiet and withdrawn and mostly preferred to sit in her room, often making an excuse that she wasn't well enough to go on duty. But neither was she really sick! She did not want to talk. Ibu Anna and the girl's room mates all tried to reason with her and draw her out of herself, but no one managed to get through to her. She got worse and didn't bother to eat.

"Dewi, won't you talk to any of us? Can't you just tell someone what's on your heart?" they pleaded in desperation. But Dewi didn't. Instead, she asked to go to her home, which was close, and here she drank disinfectant stolen from the hospital pharmacy. Her mother found her — waxy, clammy, her eyes rolling as her stomach heaved. In a collapsed state she was admitted to the hospital. But she was determined to die, she managed to tell the nurses, and shortly afterwards she did.

The hostel family was horrified. An almost breathless quietness enveloped their residence. But most upset were the girl's room mates, who came and confessed with hysterical tears that she had been practising witchcraft. When charms and fetishes were found among her belongings Anna was obliged to believe them. She felt beaten — thoroughly defeated.

"Why didn't you girls tell me before?" she demanded, "— when Dewi began to act strangely. You must have known!" She stared at them in turn, trying not to sound accusing, but desperate for an answer. They mumbled, with their eyes on their sandals: "Afraid, Ibu!" and that was all they would say.

What fear had the power to lock their lips like this? What evil presence had been sought and welcomed by Dewi in that room — until it overpowered her! Ibu Anna tried to picture Dewi caressing and murmuring over her fetishes and threatening her room mates to silence; and the girls who shared the room, their hair fairly standing on end, as they sensed something but saw nothing. The back of her own neck tingled. She had read about these things, and Kasti had talked about some of her experiences, but in the moment of crisis Anna felt helpless. They were too late. Dewi had been one of her charges — and she had failed her. The bitterness of defeat was increased by the fact that it had been going on right in the hostel, right under her eyes. Anna wondered how many more of the girls were treasuring these sinister keepsakes —

or was it only Dewi, one-time girl-friend of Chepto and of many others. Could this have been why she was so much in demand? Was it through witchcraft that she had gained her admirers? Anna was sick to think of it. She could only suspect how common fetish worship was and for what wide variety of reasons it was carried out.

Within the walls of the hospital, war against such practices was continually smouldering. Now it flared. A pastor, known for his experience in dealing with the occult, was invited to give special teaching and counselling. Everyone who fools around with these things, he declared, lays himself wide open to Satan's influence. You can get what you want from the Devil, but he claims your life in return!

In his dorm in the boys' hostel, Chepto fumbled with something that lay hidden under his mattress — the articles his mother had given him when he left home. He hadn't needed to make use of them so far, but he had kept them carefully. Now he bundled them up, the stone, the packets, even the one good for getting A grades, took them and surrendered them to the pastor.

"I don't need these any more! Do what you like with them."

When the pastor was about to leave he handed over a collection of objects to the housemother. If Ibu Anna was surprised there was no hint of it. She received the objects gravely, with fitting respect, and later had them burnt along with those that had been found in Dewi's belongings.

When she asked Chepto why he had surrendered his treasures, he told her about his former relationship with Dewi, and then, how truth had come to him through the Bible classes with Bapak Yakub.

"We have got Jesus-power to help us live. It's time I left the devil's toys alone," he finished up.

The Ibu was thoughtful. Jesus power! She liked that. She would never cease to wonder at the way His Spirit worked in people's lives. Wonder led to worship as Ibu Anna voiced a silent thank you for the student who stood before her and the encouragement that, all unknown to him, he had brought to her — just when she so badly needed it.

Then she invited Chepto to the Friday night fellowship held in the hospital chapel. Yes, he knew about it. He and Rusdi and others had listened outside the door on certain occasions, but he kept that to himself. Chepto said he would be there if he wasn't working and could find a friend. The friend turned out to be Lukas who was a regular attender.

On Friday evening, people started strolling up to the chapel in twos and threes with Bibles under their arms. While they sat waiting they began to sing unaccompanied, freely harmonizing in canons and choruses. The voices were low-pitched, the rhythm slow and folksy. Then, when it appeared everyone had gathered, a leader introduced the study material and wrote guide questions on the blackboard. To prepare their answers the young people broke up into buzz groups. Huddles of five or six scattered everywhere, and soon the pleasant hum of voices filled the big room. At first, Chepto's hands were all fingers and thumbs as he tried to locate in his Bible the verses they were talking about. But he sensed a warmth of welcome there and began to find the discussion stimulating. He slowly forgot his awkwardness. Once at ease, he couldn't help stealing a few glances around just to see who was there. His eyes fastened on a classmate in a group across the room.

It was Sri, whose home was in a country town not far from his own. Her family background was similar to his. Chepto was surprised. What had first brought her here? He didn't have any idea, but the sight of Sri, too deeply engrossed in the study to notice his wandering gaze, gave him a boost of confidence. How good it was to know there were other newcomers present. Someone in the group asked him a question which brought his attention back sharply to the study. Then a bell tinkled, and, still chattering, the groups massed together again to share their findings.

It was these people, encouraged and trained by Kasti and Anna, who visited the wards of an evening to sing and show Bible filmstrips. One such evening, not long after his introduction to the fellowship in the chapel, Chepto was on duty when a group came visiting. He and his workmates shifted beds and propped up folk with extra pillows, making sure all who wished to could see. After the film, Adih, the group leader for that night, came to speak to Chepto. Adih was a student from East Java, who came from a Christian home.

"Chep," he said. "It's one of your patients. He

wants to know more about what he has seen in the film we showed. He's got deep questions. I think you would be the one to talk to him rather than me."

"You don't say. What makes you think that?" Chepto became wary.

"Because of the way you say you were brought up. Do go and see him — the one over there with the bed cradle." Adih gave Chepto an encouraging shove in the direction of a man who was sitting, half-hidden by the metal frame arching over the bottom third of his bed and lifting the weight of the bed-cover off his injured feet. He was engrossed in the literature the nurses had left him. His cigarette, held absently in his hand, was ready to drop a couple of centimetres of ash on the sheet.

Chepto approached diffidently. But when they started to talk, it was clear that this man from one of the hill settlements around Rengas was eager for someone to explain the Bible verses on the pamphlet he was reading in terms that matched his background. He welcomed Chepto's halting attempts, and asked for more reading material to fill in the time.

There were other people like that man. For Chepto, and some of the more recent attenders of the Friday night fellowship, including Sri, this was the start of something new. People who were followers of the Lord Jesus needed to be able to say why!

Since the coup that failed, all vacation leave had been cancelled. During the months that followed —

months of civil strife, violence and uncertainty — no one had been permitted to take their holidays and, apart from a natural desire to see how their families fared, no one had been keen to do so.

There was security while they remained working in the hospital. Carry on, was the wise policy during those days — don't stick your neck out! So the decision not to allow vacations had been binding with everyone's well-being in mind.

Now, at last, it was becoming easier to travel — and safer! Chepto was preparing to visit Chimanuk again, and it bothered him. He was filled with doubts as to how the family would receive his news. They were a united family, and what they thought mattered to him. He debated with himself what line he would take.

It was a personal decision, he argued. Need the family know? Then everything could remain as it always had been. However, Chepto knew that for himself, nothing would ever be quite as it had been.

In the hostel, the problem got the usual treatment from Lukas and the inner circle of friends as they sprawled around his bunk.

"It's better to be told something directly, than to find out about it," declared Lukas. "There are ways of breaking news that are tactful and polite. How you say a thing can be almost as important as what you have to say."

"I would rather know a thing from the person concerned before I heard it whispered around the town — especially when it concerns family," was another friend's contribution.

They consulted the Bible on the subject of parents, and concluded unanimously: "Honour your parents means honour them with your confidence! That's it Chep! So long! Have a good holiday."

10 Honour your parents

It was Bapak Hamid's day off from the railway office. He was at home, dressed for relaxation in shirt and *sarung*, but busy taking stock of all the things waiting to be done around the house. He had to have it looking spick and span for Independence Day celebrations on the 17th of August. As he stood in the yard planning his day he thanked Allah that his country *was* still independent, and not in slavery to the unmentionable ideology that had captured the hearts of so many of his countrymen. He contemplated the disastrous results of that madness, its cost in human lives, the wreck of the national economy, and shuddered. He still couldn't understand how it all could have happened. He didn't think he ever would.

His family had survived the terror of the last months, and somehow they had got fed, despite the rocketing price of rice. "As rice goes, so goes the nation" was an old saying, and true enough, mused

Hamid. If the government was working for a new order and wanted to gain the confidence of the people, then it would have to start with the price of rice. They would have to stop those merchants in Jakarta forcing it up for their own gain. No wonder there were still rice riots in the capital almost daily!

But the nation's new leader was an unpretentious man who, it was said, didn't even live in the presidential palace. Instead, he preferred to stay in his own suburban home. He didn't make emotionally charged speeches either. "I can't promise you much," he had stated frankly in a nationwide broadcast heard by Bapak Hamid; but, even so, some of the ordinary things were being attended to — like roadmending. Driving a *becak* round the town was more comfortable since the holes in the highway through Chimanuk had been filled. Hamid thanked Allah again that the land he loved was returning to sanity, and that he didn't live in the city where all this political see-sawing took place, but in comparative peace in a country town.

Hamid scrutinized his home. The bamboo walls needed to be whitewashed. He wanted to exchange the cracked roof-tiles in the kitchen for some new glass ones to let in more light. But that would have to wait till he could afford it — perhaps next year. Ibu Tin had asked him to mend the rattan chairs on the porch. They looked shabby. Some of the binding strips had worked loose and hung in untidy coils. So he sat down and settled to the task, pushing and weaving the unwound strips back into place.

He thought of the children. There were only three at home now — Parmi, aged thirteen, and the two youngest boys. Rahman continued at the Islamic school maintaining his good grades, and Titi — poor Titi! Bitterness filled his thoughts. He blamed himself for her sorrow. How he regretted that they had not chosen one of the other possible suitors for her hand, instead of Harto; though at the time, everyone had been pleased with the match. The additional room they had built onto the side of the house was kept empty, for he hoped Titi and his grandson would return to it soon, now that life was becoming more settled.

And Chepto, the eldest! Hamid frowned over his handwork as he thought of Chepto. A restless boy that, to be sure; took a while to settle; turned down the best opportunity offering for his future. Hamid sighed as he split some fresh rattan strips with his knife and began to put new binding on the leg of a chair. Chepto had been a worry to him, but finally he had found some useful work to keep himself out of mischief. Hamid was relieved about that.

In these days, the young people faced big temptations and frustrations. Education — everyone was scrambling for it; but work, really worthwhile work, was as scarce as ever.

His son's last note from Rengas had been to let the family know that his much overdue vacation had been granted. In fact, they were expecting him in Chimanuk any day. Hamid finished replacing the old binding on the last of the chairs and surveyed them with satisfaction. He decided to save

the whitewashing until his son had come to share
the task with him.

Towards evening, a crowded minibus pulled up
outside Bapak Hamid's house. Before Chepto could
ease himself out from where he was wedged among
the other passengers, his two young brothers were
at the roadside, fighting to carry his small bundle of
possessions. A warmth of affection for his family
filled him as he greeted them. His father was
looking as lean and immaculate as always, his
cheeks perhaps a little more hollow under his high
cheek bones. His mother had put on her best *sarung*
which she hardly ever wore, and Parmi had taken
her thick schoolgirl pigtail and coiled it up in a
clever arrangement on the top of her head. The
effect was as she meant it to be — quite grown up.

That night, another of Ibu Tin's chickens met its
end, and appeared with the rice and vegetables on
the tables. They sat around on the porch to eat.
How nice it was to use fingers again after the "cold
steel" of the hostel cutlery! And how much nicer
everything tasted!

This was their first meeting as a family since
before the attempted coup, the aftermath of which
had turned the country upside down. Hamid
relished the political details and was enthusiastic at
the hard-line justice still being meted out to the
rebels. He wanted to talk about it, but Chepto did
his best politely to discourage him. Chepto wanted
to enjoy the simple welcome and its recognition of
his having found a worthwhile job and a place to
study. Yet, even though he was within the intimacy

of the family circle, which was normally the easiest place in the world to relax, Chepto was not at ease. He remained tense and aloof, thinking all the time about how to tell Bapak Hamid his most important news. He had to tell him. No matter what his father's reaction, Chepto was sure he would prefer to know. He remembered the talk with the hostel boys and that helped. Honour your parents means to be honest with them.

The meal was over. The younger boys went in to sleep. Ibu Tin and Parmi were in the kitchen preparing the railway station snacks. Bapak Hamid and his eldest son sat on the porch in silence. Chepto started counting the little lizards that clung sleepily to the walls. He recalled the occasion when he had last spoken alone with his father. It was when he had given over Uncle Hasan's offer of an education to his younger brother Rahman. His father had been keenly disappointed. And now, for the second time, he was about to bring deep disappointment to him. He would have given almost anything to avoid it. He pulled his feet in under his *sarung* — the mosquitoes were savage — and puffed clove smoke.

Hamid broke the silence.

"It looks as though you have found a purpose that appeals to you in Rengas, my son. I can't tell you how pleased your mother and I are."

Chepto winced. In his heart he said; "God, heavenly Father, you know what my father here is like. Help me to use the words that will be right for him." Aloud, he heard himself saying:

"Father, I have found more than that."

"Indeed!" Hamid turned to his son expectantly. Perhaps he had laid eyes on a future wife, he thought. It wasn't too soon ...

"I have become a Christian." It just slid out, flat and expressionless. Chepto could not look at his father. He sat stiffly, gazing ahead at the road and the shadow of "mother's *warung*" in the moonlight. Other students who had taken the same step flocked to his mind. Ketut from Bali whose father had stopped writing to him; Ratih, who had been chased out of her home; Sri, his classmate, whose family pretended that she didn't exist ... and he waited.

Chepto heard his father draw in his breath. Bapak Hamid had also concentrated his gaze on the silhouette of the little *warung*. His mind retraced the lines of development in his ancestral tree; the generations of unbroken and exemplary loyalty to another tradition; and he wondered what he had done wrong, that a son of his should want to be different.

At last, he spoke quite quietly:

"There has never been anyone in our family who followed the way you have chosen." Chepto could not see the hurt and puzzlement in his eyes because his father wasn't looking at him, and the light was dim, but it was there in his voice.

Then Hamid gripped the sides of this chair and turned to the younger man and said: "But we cannot live in the past. This is the new order. In this nation everyone is free to worship God as he sees fit. Isn't that the essence of the *Panca Sila?*"[1] Chepto nodded, acknowledging the first of five basic principles undergirding the constitution of his nation. Every school child knew these — it was their first lesson in citizenship.

"If you must choose this way," his father continued with quiet intensity, "if you wish to become a Christian, then I have only one thing to add. See that you are a good one!"

How like Bapak Hamid! In the quiet of his greatly-relieved heart Chepto gave thanks for his father's integrity.

During the vacation, Chepto helped whitewash the house, replaced leaky roof tiles, and generally tried to act with special thoughtfulness. He badly wanted to show his family that what he had done didn't make any difference in the family circle; that he still loved them as he had always done — in fact more so. But relationships weren't quite natural.

He came across his mother shedding tears in the kitchen. She pleaded with him: "How shall I tell our relations?" Uncle Hasan was her big worry, but she had others on her mind too. "What will our friends and neighbours think? And the rest of the town? I feel so ashamed. How could you do this to us?"

Chepto longed to be able to comfort her, but Ibu Tin would not be comforted. She sat down on a

---

[1] *Panca Sila* (pr. pancha sila) — literally 'five principles', this is the philosophical preface to the constitution, expressing the basic political beliefs of the nation: Belief in the one supreme god; just and civilized humanity; unity of Indonesia; democracy; social justice.

stool, silently dabbing her eyes with the end of her *sarung*, and Chepto did not know what to say to her. He was certain that when the first shock was over, she would take her cue from his father and not exclude her firstborn from her life. But it was hard!

11 Prisoners at Pujen

"It's like being bankrupt and not knowing that you are. That's just about the state we are in." The voice was rasping as it rose above the background of complaining chatter coming from students gathered in a group in the men's hostel.

"You could be right there, mate!" Another voice took over. "But I say we are more like a jeep running downhill backwards, out of control. And then it stops — right at the edge of a chasm. It's a miracle!" The chatter quietened as the new voice captured their interest. The speaker continued: "Yes, that about describes the country at the time of the coup that misfired. Now the jeep is starting slowly to climb the hill again in first gear. That's us today, making a fresh start, very slowly, but going forward." His body was swaying and his voice began to rise in a high-pitched crescendo. "Yes! We are going forward. We are not looking back into the chasm!" The speaker stopped for breath. Everyone was laughing now, and there were cries of approval at this off-the-cuff speech. It was intended to encourage students at the hospital who had just received the news that this month only a percentage of their allowance could be paid.

Chepto remembered his brother-in-law's jeers about the money he earned being scarcely enough to keep a person in soap and toothpaste. It was hard to find any to buy anyhow!

It wasn't just the hospital. Every institution was battling with its own economic problems. Not one remained untouched, and some had been forced to close their doors. The situation everywhere in Rengas was simply a reflection of the wider national struggle.

Firms in the habit of subsidizing medical care costs for their employees were unable to do so. People put off coming for help unless they were in a desperate condition, afraid that they would not be able to meet the minimal costs of hospital care. The midwives made wry jokes about mothers who preferred to give birth at home, rather than have to negotiate the bumpy surface of Rekso Road.

Pharmacy cupboards were often bare.

To keep the operating room functioning, nurses would spend their free time searching the shops of Rengas for sewing thread, then preparing and sterilizing it for skin sutures in surgery. All soiled dressings they soaked, washed and resterilized for further use. Every centimetre of gauze was precious. Nothing was wasted.

And the service continued. For those determined to keep on ministering to a community's need, it became a challenge to see how much could be done with next to nothing for their equipment.

It was during this period that a foreign guest came with an offer of help. After he had been shown around he became critical of general standards of practice. His host, Dr. Hartono, could only have been more discouraged than pleased, for he countered:

"I'm sorry you feel like that. Yes — we know our standards are not the best. That's one of our problems. But we can't be downhearted. We praise God that we are functioning at all! You see," he added drily, "there will always be different ways of looking at the same thing."

But events *had* taken a turn, and the new direction was forward. Although few of those involved in the day-by-day struggle to keep going were yet aware of it, imperceptibly the rebuilding of a nation had begun.

It was a typical hospital morning. There was a lull in the bustle in the wards. The doctors had finished their rounds, the beds were tidy rows, and the whole place smelled faintly of fresh disinfectant. Where Chepto was currently working the charge nurse had gone off to a staff meeting, and the nurses on duty were marking charts and writing up reports in the ward office — and talking. If fewer and fewer people could afford to be treated, and the hospital just kept on getting emptier, how would they, the students, ever be able to complete their training? Could a hospital be forced to close its doors? Such a wild idea didn't bear thinking about, so someone abruptly changed the subject.

"Have any of you seen the new patient in men's medical ward?"

"Which new patient? What about him?" several voices demanded.

"They say the government is paying his bill."

"Oh? Which patient do you mean?" more voices were questioning.

"Badu is his name. There is a guard with him — that fellow in uniform who sits out in the sun and smokes and reads all day."

"What's he done?" The group were getting really curious, which was just what their informant wanted.

"He's from Pujen!" the informant volunteered with a knowing inflection in his voice. This statement caused the report writers and chart markers to stop with ball-points poised.

"You mean the political prison! The hospital will be waiting for that bill to be settled till everyone has forgotten about it."

"How did he get from Pujen to here?" someone wanted to know.

"When it was plain that the man was really ill and needed to go to hospital, they asked him which one he preferred. He used to live around here before he was arrested, so he said he wanted to come to Immanuel. His wife can visit him easily. She lives in Prak Lane!"

Chepto looked up quickly, then tried to appear casual. Would he never be able to forget that name?

He went on marking charts vigorously, but his heart was thumping. He felt sure the others would notice it too, because of the way his white overall was bouncing where it covered his chest. So he started to move about the ward looking for other things that might need doing. Later, there was a reason to visit men's medical, and while there, he made a point of studying the prisoner from a distance.

He observed a quite ordinary-looking middle-aged man with graying hair. The man wore a faded *sarung* and lay on top of his bed. He appeared to be dozing. The patient wasn't communicating, the nurse told Chepto. He spoke only when it was necessary.

It was Bapak Yakub who finally succeeded in penetrating the silent man's reserve and finding out something about him. In Pujen prison where he had come from, there were hundreds of people. Behind its forbidding walls Badu, the Communist, had begun to long for God. Now, when there was someone who was willing to spend time telling him about God, that person found a ready listener. Bapak Yakub visited him often, and, in typical unhurried style, they would spend whole afternoons just exchanging thoughts, till Badu's illness began to respond to treatment and he recovered. Before he had to return to Pujen he asked to be baptized. A special offering in the Sunday chapel service at hospital purchased a Bible for him, and then Badu stepped back into prison determined to minister on the inside.

"In there, we fellows have all day to study God's word," he said almost gaily as he and the guard left the hospital. He confessed that he wasn't very learned, but that there were others in Pujen a lot better educated than he was who shared his interest. They would help each other.

The Friday night fellowship members prayed for Badu and his self-appointed ministry in his unusual parish, but they did not really expect to hear anything more from one who was a prisoner.

Weeks passed. Then Bapak Yakub received a note from the prison. As he read and reread the letter he could hardly believe his eyes. Would the hospital be willing to share a ministry among the prisoners with a Christian university group on an alternate weekly basis? They couldn't let that request go by. Despite shift duty they would manage something between them.

No one ever really knew how the prison church came into being. But it was there — and growing, like a plant grows in a rocky cleft, thriving in unlikely surroundings because its roots are tapping some hidden source of nourishment.

On the inside, Badu was waiting. True to his promise, he was encouraging and reading from his Bible to anyone who would hear him. He had got into trouble for being over-enthusiastic and, as some other inmates claimed, upsetting the peace. But he took it all calmly, as something about which no one should be surprised.

Time hung heavily on the hands of those inside, for there were few facilities and a great many prisoners. So, to help fill the blank days, Badu's friends managed to find some English language magazines which they brought in. Some of the prisoners were studying English, directed by those among them who had formerly been teachers of English. But, best of all, each time a group of students visited the prison for a worship service they brought new Bibles to use, and left them there. Not a great number could be left this way — not more than two or three each visit; but the ones that were left got well-thumbed as they were read and reread, and through them, God nourished his expanding church inside Pujen.

By the time Chepto was able to join a group for Pujen, Badu reckoned there were at least fifty persons awaiting permission from the prison governor to be baptized.

Chepto's group drove to the city limits. The prison wasn't hard to find. It was an ancient fortress, a legacy from Dutch colonial days before independence. For years it had been only partly used, but now, suddenly, since the political upheaval, it was housing an exploding population.

They parked the hospital vehicle under Pujen's massive, mouldy walls. Through its doors and inside they were required to show their special passes to be checked off — eight in all. Then they trailed after the guard along a dark passage, until finally, they came into a huge, stonewalled room. It was completely bare, except for about one hundred men sitting crosslegged on the floor.

The visitors also went to sit on the floor, but

when the prisoners saw that some of the students who had come were girls, a few of them went out and returned with some battered hemp mats, the kind used for sleeping on, and laid them over the stone surface.

The prisoners all looked the same — gaunt, shabby, a mass of unkempt brown faces, the hungry gaze of two hundred eyes. But among them there were teenagers, university professors, ex-army men, clerks and labourers — every kind of citizen! They were the forgotten men, wanting to live, yet expecting to die.

Taken aback at what they found, the visitors began to wonder what they were doing inside this great, bleak room, and why they had dared to think anything they might have to say could mean very much to all these men. They were embarrassed and self-conscious. Their former confidence seemed to have evaporated. However, they had to carry on. Lukas, who had often preached in the hospital wards, did so here; Chepto told what it meant to him to be a follower of Jesus, and the choir taught some songs. Then, just when one would have expected the meeting to conclude, the prisoners started to do some speaking of their own. At first, one or two stood up, then one after the other they rose, competing for the chance to express in their own words what they too believed; to sing or recite a Bible verse that had special meaning for them. It was the audience that was leading in a wonderful, joyful fellowship, until a guard motioned them to stop.

The hospital team stood speechless at the takeover. One of the girls was wiping tears from her cheeks as Lukas, who had somehow found his usual presence of mind again, formally closed the meeting. Then the "forgotten men" started to shuffle out. This was the limited opportunity for the visitors to mix with those inside on a one-to-one basis. The prisoners were slowly making their way towards the exit, when a fellow in the crowd brushed against Chepto.

"How is Titi?" the man asked in a casual whisper.

"Titi?" He's mistaken me for someone else, thought Chepto. "What is Titi to you?" he asked.

"Titi, daughter of Hamid — she's my wife!" Chepto's mouth gaped. Words just wouldn't come out. He looked at the figure standing before him, ungroomed, with threadbare clothes hanging on it. The scarecrows they used to put in the rice fields at Chimanuk flashed before his mind. But there was no doubt about that face.

"You are Harto!" he managed finally. Harto said nothing, but he looked everything — questioning, beseeching.

"Titi's all right," mumbled Chepto.

"And the baby?"

"All right too," he mumbled again. The prisoners were being hustled by guards grown impatient at the delay, and Harto was carried along and out with the crowd. Chepto and the team from the hospital were escorted back down the long corridor that smelt of damp and mould. They counted themselves past the sentry at the door — eight souls all present and correct — and blinked in the glorious, bright sun of freedom.

So Harto was alive if not exactly well, when they had supposed him dead! A strange emotion welled up in Chepto's heart. He was not overjoyed that his sister's husband lived. He had been abrupt and rude, and it wasn't because of the shock of discovery, although that was bad enough. Nor was it the fact of Harto's unmentionable past associations. That was secondary! Chepto recognized again the antipathy he had always felt towards his brother-in-law. He was still resentful — but ashamed of it.

The team members sat swaying in the back of the jeep as it ground noisily home to the hospital. Chepto was silent and scowling. He knew that he could never go back to visit the prison unless his attitude towards Harto changed.

"O God," he thought. "You who loved this crazy world so much that You sent Jesus here — help me to love Harto. Please give me an opportunity to go back to the prison and talk to him."

The young people continued their two-weekly visits to Pujen prison, making friends and bringing encouragement to the church on the inside. Chepto's turn came around again. Back in the great stone-walled room, he searched the faces of those sitting cross-legged before him, looking for Harto. A sea of faces met his gaze; they all looked the same; it was like searching the ocean. Well, if he couldn't see Harto, Harto would certainly have no excuse for not seeing him. He stopped peering into the crowd, afraid of drawing attention to himself. Afterwards, when the meeting broke up, Chepto made a point of standing apart a little, not too obviously he hoped, and waited. The men started to move around, and after a few seconds that seemed like hours, Harto emerged. Chepto spoke first.

"Harto! Titi and your son are well. His name is Jus. They are living at home." The words came quickly, with relief and yes — even joy.

"Thank God! We were wrong Chep. The Communist way brought disaster," confessed Harto. Chepto looked hard at him and wondered if Harto believed the Communist way was wrong only because it had ended in disaster — like the man who has backed the unlucky bird in a cock-fight and lost his money. Were they wrong only because they had failed? He steered Harto over to a slightly quieter part of the room.

"We were all wrong," he said. "There is no one right. Every one of us needs to be made clean from our wrongness through Jesus, the Son of God. I have been one of His followers for several months. What about you? What stage are you at?"

"Learning," Harto replied cautiously. "I've been coming here for a while now. We study the Bible most days — there isn't much else to study! But isn't it amazing that God should be in this place! And care about us! By the time they have the governor's permission to be baptized, I will be ready too." They were silent, but not for long. The guards were calling out for dismissal.

"Look after Titi and the baby till I get back. Teach her what we share. I don't know what will happen to us. Sometimes we are afraid for the future, but I'm not afraid of dying — not now."

The all-too-brief free time was over, and the party from the hospital was obliged to leave once more.

Soon after that, a big reshuffle occurred in the world of prisoners, as the government pursued justice and the revival of political normality. Some prisoners were judged as mild offenders or as misled, and they were released with a warning. Others were found guilty of crimes against the state and shifted to a different prison. A third group were removed to isolated Eastern atolls to complete their sentence in banishment, and Harto went with them. Chepto had no further opportunity to visit him.

12 *Good news in Chimanuk*

Chepto wrote to Titi telling her how they had found Harto in the prison. He avoided details about the prisoners, feeling that she had enough to concern her without getting upset about conditions she was powerless to change. Nor did he mention Harto's search for God. That must wait for a face-to-face meeting when Titi's questions could be answered directly.

As he worked around the hospital, Chepto found his thoughts often focussing on Ibu Tin and Bapak Hamid and the family. He wished they could meet some of his special friends at the hospital. But how? Neither party had a reason, or the funds, to travel. How could he work it so that the family had a chance to know what his new friends were really like. He was sure that if they did know, they would be able to accept the way he had chosen more easily. Especially his mother! She had been the most upset. She just didn't know anyone outside of her family and her circle in Chimanuk. Chepto felt almost certain that she had never even met any Christians.

And then a patient solved the problem for him. She had been watching a film about the life of Jesus shown on the wards one evening, and it had touched her heart deeply. The following day, she was bursting with enthusiasm about it.

"Why, that's what I believe too!" she told Chepto with wonder. "But how clearly and simply your friends explained everything. I've never heard it so plainly before. Fancy having to come to hospital and be flat on your back before you really understand what you believe!" and her delight bubbled into giggles at the very idea.

Chepto made a mental note. I must tell this to Kasti, he thought. She was doing the talking that night. Then he grinned at the lady, his eyes conveying the message, "please go on, I'm listening."

"I've thought of a splendid plan," she continued. "Tell your friends to come to my home when I'm well, and we will arrange for them to talk to the young people at my church."

That triggered it! Why not go to the church at Chimanuk as well? And why not the home towns of other students, if there was a church, and if it was possible? The ideas started to explode like crackers inside his head, and he had to share them quickly. Lukas thought it was first rate. So did Adih. Ibu Anna saw a sign of growing maturity in the concern to develop this new challenge. Bapak Yakub was pleased if cautious. It was something he had always hoped for. "But, well," as he said in his usual non-committal way, "a group of young people descending on a community for a couple of nights was a delight that would take a bit of handling."

They wrote off to Pastor Jonas in Chimanuk. And before there had been time to think much more about it, Chepto found himself in charge of operations, because it was his home town that was being visited.

Then the doubts started to whittle away his enthusiasm. He had only once seen inside the church building where Pastor Jonas ministered — and that had been to write an examination paper! The people of Chimanuk knew him only as the son of Hamid the railway clerk, an industrious man whose family was respected for its loyalty to the traditions of Islam. But as plans got under way, his uncertainties were soon being replaced with great expectations.

One Saturday morning, the plans burst into action. For transport, the group were to use a hospital station wagon that had been given specially with operations like this in mind. Its long, blue body pulled up outside the girls' hostel for loading.

They were taking their own food, so that no host family would cut themselves short on behalf of the guests. It was basic stuff, simply what they would have eaten had they been remaining in the hostel for the weekend. The girls measured out the rice ration — half a kilo per person per day, the standard allowance. It filled two round cane baskets at the back of the vehicle. One of the girls buried some eggs in the rice for safe travel, while another piled vegetables on top. They tucked in some dried fish and slabs of yellow soy bean cake wrapped in banana leaf. A few handfuls of red peppers for flavour completed the food require- ments, but still they went on adding. A blackboard, some home-made visuals aids, a box of books and Bibles to sell, a minimum of personal luggage, some pillows and a full can of petrol. This was a practical gesture from Dr. Hartono who knew that petrol was still in uncertain supply. "Don't leave it behind, whatever you do," he cautioned. There were two alternatives that had to be avoided at all costs — black market prices which none of them could afford, or being stranded indefinitely when they were expected for duty.

Five girls, three fellows, a member of staff — that trip it happened to be Sister Lyn who was free — and the driver, clambered aboard the station wagon. It edged out into Rekso Road, almost nudging some of the smaller vehicles, nosed its way slowly across the city, wound through the mountain pass and down to the plain.

That evening, after welcomes, the party split up for billeting. The five girls were all together in one home sharing a family-size bed platform complete with mosquito net, but the boys ended up on mats in an outbuilding. Nobody minded. After the long, hot journey they would sleep soundly anywhere.

The party had arranged to do their cooking themselves, rather than burden a local family with such a large assignment. Soon, amid much action and chatter, the steam began to rise from the rice cooker and the tantalizing smell of dried fish simmering and bean cake sizzling filled their hostess's kitchen.

Once preparations for the evening meal were well under control, Chepto slipped away from the scene of action. He walked along the road. There were still plenty of people about, but no one recognized him. Arriving at the church, he turned into the pathway that led past its wall to the cottage behind. There in the porch was the little table with the cloth and the flowers on it — the sign that spoke welcome everywhere. The woven bamboo walls, like those of his own home, were flaky with many plasterings of whitewash. It looked dark inside. Chepto stepped onto the porch and called out the typical Sundanese greeting: "Punten! Excuse me!" His voice was a high-pitched drawl.

"You are invited to enter," a voice called back. Then its owner appeared in the doorway carrying an unlit pressure lamp. Only the new houses in Chimanuk boasted electricity.

"Bapak Jonas, do you remember me?" The pastor peered at his guest in the half light, but it was only a moment before he put down the lamp and, with a big smile, stretched out his hands.

"Yes, of course I do. You are Hamid's son. Welcome." How could he forget that tall, morose-looking lad with his stand-up, wavy hair who had drifted into the church that day — could it be two years ago? At least. So much had happened since then, it seemed more like four. He beamed again at

Chepto.

"Do you remember that day when you sat the examination in the church over there with all the others?" Chepto nodded. He wasn't likely to forget it.

"I was hoping to choose a good group of recruits for Immanuel hospital, and you were the best I could do." There was something comical about Pastor Jonas's face. Chepto began to grin as the pastor continued: "I told Bapak Yakub to expect several candidates from this area, and got one." Chepto's grin expanded, and then they were both laughing.

"I was embarrassed, I tell you. But God saw further than Bapak Jonas. He knew who He was choosing." The pastor looked Chepto up and down and motioned him to one of the rattan chairs. Then he put the pressure lamp on the table and started to light it.

"Well, you will soon be meeting our young people. This is a unique occasion. We don't have so many regulars, but tonight I think there may be some who are there to satisfy their curiosity — and this will be good. I will come and introduce you and your friends, and then it's over to you." His eyes twinkled. Jonas enjoyed young people.

"Yes, we would like you to do that," Chepto replied. While the lamp was being pumped to a bright glow, he thought about what Bapak Jonas had said just then, when they were laughing together.

"Bapak," he began, "I just took a chance with

that entrance examination. I thought, pass or fail, it can't matter. It's what Allah wills. He has decided my fate! When I passed, sure — it was His will all right, but in a way I did not understand then. He did know who He was choosing. He wanted me to go to the hospital where I would hear about Him. Then when trouble came and I needed help really badly, I knew where to find it."

Jonas's eyes gave a knowing sparkle, and the smile crinkled his wrinkly face again. He started to speak as though he was sharing a secret. "It can be like that when you look back. Sometimes you can see how all along, God has been planning for you in love. 'It's God who has made us what we are, and given us new lives from Jesus, so that we may carry out those things that He has planned for us.'"[1]

Chepto didn't have anything to say to that. His vision hadn't begun to stretch much beyond the present.

"He has His purpose for each one of us," said Bapak Jonas.

"Do you think so? I can't see past graduation at this stage. It's not far off now." They would really have to get down to preparation after this trip was over, he thought.

"You will know what God's purpose for you is when the time is right. He will show you what He wants you to do." Jonas was just beginning to warm to a subject dear to him, and had forgotten the

---

[1] Ephesians 2:10

hour, but Chepto felt that he had quite enough on his hands for the next few months without getting too concerned about what lay beyond. It was time to return to the others and to get ready for the evening programme. His attention had begun to wander and he only half heard the next bit.

"Then, if you truly want to honour Him with all your heart you will choose the right way," concluded Bapak Jonas as his guest excused himself and went back to share the meal his mates had prepared.

That night, and the following morning, the little church was full. Some of the hospital young people helped with Sunday School or took part in the worship service. Others set up a stall in the church yard. They found a shady spot under a spreading mango tree. There they laid a *sarung* across a couple of benches and arranged the books and Bibles on top. The brightly-coloured dust-jackets made a gay patchwork against the more sombre tones of the *sarung*. After the service, the mini-crowd swarmed around, and the book supplies the students had brought were soon sold out. Cash was short, so the people bartered with rice, fruit and live chickens, all of which was taken back to the hostel at Immanuel hospital and converted into cash again.

In country towns like Chimanuk there was nowhere to buy such things as Bibles. Distribution was the problem, Bapak Jonas explained, and a supply that never managed to catch up with the demand.

In the afternoon, Chepto took two friends, Adih

and Sri, along to his home. Adih was Javanese, and so was Ibu Tin. She had been born and reared in the eastern part of the island of Java, and liked nothing better than a chat in the language of her girlhood, instead of the Sundanese tongue usually spoken at home with her family.

When the trio arrived they found her alone, lying on the sleeping platform in the darkest part of the house with a cold compress on her forehead. No need to get up, they quickly assured her, as Ibu Tin began to fuss. "Just tired," she said, and lay back. So they sat on the platform beside her, which was the last way Ibu Tin would ever have expected to receive guests in her house. But she submitted gratefully.

Adih had a way with him which allowed him to be comfortable with people in whatever situation he found them, and made them feel the same. They started to chat about Ibu Tin's home area in the east, about the hospital, their families, God, His love for people — and Ibu Tin's heart was touched. Her attitude softened, and before they left she was calling Adih "My son ...", a sure sign of acceptance. His warmth and naturalness had delighted her. They gave her a New Testament which she received graciously as the gift of a friend, and promised to read.

And Bapak Hamid — where was he? Why wasn't he there? Chepto put off inquiring as long as he could, because he had an idea what the answer was going to be. It wasn't till the end of the visit, when they were about to go, that he found out. His father had chosen to be absent. He could not bring himself to associate with the visitors, and this was the most dignified way of escaping what for him would have been a confrontation! He would rather withdraw than risk appearing other than gracious and polite. Chepto knew that this was his father's way of making sure everyone understood that no matter what others did, his lifelong loyalty to the traditions of his family would remain unchallenged.

His father's attitude caused Chepto's enthusiasm to wilt. Perhaps it also explained why his mother had been "just tired" when they arrived at the house — really she had been hiding her distress over the break in family unity. Honour to parents — many times Chepto and his mates had thrashed out this, along with other matters, in hostel discussions. Give them your confidence; show them that nothing has changed your love and respect for them; were some of their conclusions. But where there was no communication, how could you? How could you possibly show them anything?

Chepto remembered the last talk with his father.

"We cannot live in the past," Hamid had said. "This is the new order ... everyone is free to worship God as he sees fit." With his mind Hamid had acknowledged the freedom of a new order, but his heart was buried in the old. Chepto felt empty. He had lost something precious, a relationship that would never be the same again. Grief was a new emotion for him, and he had to keep it hidden for the remainder of the weekend. The rest of the group were in high spirits over the welcome they had received from the Chimanuk church and the new friends they had gained. He could not intrude just then with his personal sorrow.

There wasn't much time left to spend with Titi. She was eager to hear further news about Harto, but there was no more to be told. She was living at home again, in the extra room that had been built for them. She enjoyed caring for her small son, and went on hoping for her husband's return after his sentence had been served. When Chepto told her of Harto's desire to become a Christian, she insisted on taking lessons herself so that they could be a truly united family. What a girl! thought Chepto. He could not help admiring his sister's vision and courage, and arranged for her to visit Bapak Jonas. The pastor promised to help her, and Titi promised to teach Parmi.

So Titi became an inquirer. There were often inquiries these days — more than Bapak Jonas could ever remember in all his years of pastoring.

"Do you think some people come here to save their skins, just so they won't be labelled Communists?" It was a question Chepto couldn't help asking when he went back to make arrangements for Titi's instruction. Bapak Jonas wrinkled his forehead and took a long time to answer.

"Maybe," he said finally. His voice showed no surprise. "But, if people are prepared to listen, shouldn't we tell them the good news from God?"

The terror, apprehension and uncertainty that had once filled the land was less now. The savage reprisals had run full circle and had ceased. All that had happened had been God's opportunity, Bapak Jonas was sure. How he wished that the church had many more leaders able to take hold of that opportunity — leaders who could teach others from the Word of God, when there were so many "others" ready to be taught.

13 A question of choice

Back at the hospital, Chepto had to set aside his private griefs and hopes concerning his family for an all-out effort to grasp the immediate goal. During the weeks that lay ahead, he and his classmates would need to concentrate all their attention on the business of graduating.

Graduation! It was the occasion every student dreamed about. And "Finals" was the discriminating process every student dreaded! For those who would gain the glory of the former, there was no way round the latter. So — it was down to serious slog for them all.

Lights began to burn every night in the tutorial block. Some people liked to study in groups; knowledge had a way of sinking in more easily when aired and shared among contemporaries. Others preferred private revision. Elbows propped up heads as they sat and pored over the piles of handwritten notes they had accumulated during three years of lectures. Text books had become scarce, and were held in the library to be used only under supervision.

Teachers returned in the evenings for special tutorials, and Sister Lyn held practical demonstrations and question-answer sessions in the operating room block.

Chepto attended one of these. Inside the large, pale-green room he stood under the adjustable lamp that hung suspended from the ceiling, and watched Sister Lyn demonstrate. He was conscious again of the faint but permeating smell of ether that no one could ever quite get rid of. Memories came flooding back — Uncle Waji, Dr. Daniel, Hasanah and the rest.

He had enjoyed working here. In this place he had first become aware of a new dimension to caring for sick people. The surgical team had been aiming for a healing that meant more than merely restored bodily health.

Here too he had begun to like doing medical work for its own sake. Up till then, he had done the things he had to do in order to gain the diploma he wanted so much. What a crazy character, he thought to himself. And now that diploma was within clutching distance.

Whenever anyone wasn't studying, the conversation topic that came top of the popularity poll was future plans. Moving in on almost any group a person was likely to hear the stock question:

"What are you going to do when this is over?" But there was no stock answer.

"We're returning to North Sumatra as soon as

the church up there sends our fares. They sponsored us to come here so that we would work in their hospital afterwards." The speakers were two girls who had frequently helped Kasti with ward evangelism, and now wanted to do the same back in their home area.

"Your minds have been made up for you then?"

"Sort of. We're sad to have to leave so soon. We'll miss the fellowship, but they need us up there." They would go by boat from Jakarta to Medan, and then inland. It was a trip of several days.

"It's the same for me," a fellow added. "My church in Kalimantan sent me. There's a lot of health problems in the interior of my island, not much medicine, and no resident doctors. Some clinics have had to close, but I hope I can help open them again." Others wanted to staff policlinics[1] offering basic medical services in rural areas, while the army medical corps was a popular preference with the boys.

"What about you, Rusdi?" Chepto turned to his long-time friend.

"I shall go home," was the decisive reply. But Rusdi lived close, only a couple of hours' journey away. "There's room for another nurse in the policlinic that serves the rubber plantation there."

---

[1] *Policlinic* — a multi-purpose clinic for basic medical needs, and a feature of Indonesian medical coverage. In many country places these are administered wholly by nurses who are skilled in recognizing and treating local conditions. A doctor visits at stated intervals. Patients who cannot be handled at the policlinic are referred to the nearest hospital. There are still some areas where this means a journey of several days.

"Pill-pusher! You've got it sewn up well," the others chorused.

"That's right! It's sure money — better than here by a long way. The plantation is the party that pays, you see — not the workers that get treated. And if the cash runs out I'll take rice for payment, or whatever they have — anything will do." He paused, looking pleased with himself.

"And you Chep, what about you?" asked Rusdi.

"I wish I was sure." Chepto spoke thoughtfully and his expression was grave. He was sorry that student days were almost over. They would soon all be separating to go their various ways. He was finding thought about the future difficult.

"Well, what about you and Sri?" Rusdi's voice was probing, and Chepto just off guard enough to hesitate for an answer. He had got to know Sri during these past months, as they had been learning together with others as new as themselves about following Jesus, and again when working together on the programme for the Chimanuk weekend. He tried to play down this growing friendship with his classmate, hoping none of the more gossipy types around the hostel would notice. There was nothing like a few long tongues to foul up developments of this sort.

"Not sure about that either," Chepto replied at last. "Perhaps you had better ask Sri!" He laughed lightly at his friend's obvious disappointment and then became serious again. "It's for real, Rusdi! And, if you want to know, I'm interested in joining the army, because if I could get in there, Sri and I could think about getting married. There would be living quarters along with the job. Anyhow, I'm trying. But we have to get this exam first!"

The Sunday before the big event, Bapak Yakub prayed for the class of finalists in chapel: "Help them to remember all that they have faithfully studied." That was a reasonable request, thought Chepto as he sat in the pew. "And Lord, just prompt them to look for your signposts as they step out into the future." With feeling Chepto echoed the Amen to that too.

Finals were conducted orally by a panel of examiners. This group visited each school of nursing in the Rengas area in turn, and each finalist had to face all eight members. After three tense days of dialogue the panel held a meeting, and then the candidates learned who had been successful and who had not.

"Anyone who passes along to the end of that line-up without getting in a muddle deserves to graduate," commented one candidate.

"By that time you're so limp that it's only the starch in your uniform that's holding you up," complained another.

"A real play act!" someone else growled. "Am I glad that's over!"

The three-day marathon ended with an evening of ceremony and speeches followed by food and fun. The school block was lit up and decorated with flowers. The folding glass doors all along its northern face were opened out to their fullest so that people were free to move around. The auditorium overflowed with visitors, the friends and families of graduates, distinguished guests, hospital personnel, and the simply curious who drifted in from Rekso Road and out again. The guests spilled over onto the patio that ran the full length of the building, and down the steps onto the grass and the driveway beyond. Their voices and laughter, mingled with the fragrance of clove smoke and body perfumes, drifted out into the warm night.

It was a family celebration. Even those graduates whose families were not near enough to be able to accept the invitation, found themselves drawn into the family circles of others.

The ceremony was about to begin. People entered the auditorium to find seats, and the chatter hushed as tutors, Dr. Hartono, Bapak Yakub and others took their places on the dais. Then the student body rose to sing a hymn as the procession of graduates entered. Every head turned to see the girls with stiffly-starched caps perched like butterflies on their shining black coiffures, and the boys with knife creases in their trousers the like of which would not be seen again.

From her place on the dais with the other teachers, Sister Lyn sat watching. Her eyes swept over each student in turn. "How nice they look!" she thought. They passed by below her one by one, to find their places in the block of seats set aside for them. "How young, how vital and expectant! What do the days ahead hold for each one?" After they passed, she settled back more easily in her own seat. "Now for all the *sambutan!*" she said to herself. "We might do better with a few less of these welcome speeches!"

As time passed, and the welcomes continued, her mind went back to the time when she first came to the hospital. It was because Dr. Hartono had asked for help from the missionary organization to which she belonged. At their first meeting the doctor had shared some of his vision for the outreach of Immanuel Hospital. She remembered a dynamic little man seated in an untidy office, and even with the distance of a vast paper-strewn desk separating them, she had felt his dynamism radiate towards her. He came to the point immediately.

"We need upgrading," he had said, clipping his words short, his eyes sparkling. "Upgrading in medical and nursing care; upgrading spiritually, so that people will find a wholeness here." His direct gaze seemed to imply — do you really understand what I am getting at? Have I made myself clear? He had. When Dr. Hartono spoke about something that was close to his heart, it wasn't hard to see as he saw. But he wasn't so clear concerning the detail.

"What do you have in mind for me, now that I have come?" Sister Lyn had asked a little uncertainly. He had looked at her with just a trace of surprise, shrugged his shoulders in a don't quite know gesture, and said; "The nurses, please — teach them something." So it had been over to her. She had begun to wonder wherever she would start and however she would fit in to a going concern like the hospital, when he had added: "You will start in the operating room, of course. Dr. Daniel is hoping for that." And so, that is where she had begun.

Working with other staff to modernize methods and update techniques, working to improve the teaching and training programme; seeing young people become skilled and move off; welcoming others waiting to be trained to fill their places and then move off too — this was the student scene.

It was thrilling to have a part in equipping young folk who would serve needy communities in far-flung areas of the nation. But sometimes the needs of the home base were overlooked. They also needed to train folk who would *not* move off. Sister Lyn knew that her time at the hospital was limited; that she must try to do what she came to do, teach others, and go. Work yourself out of a job, was the realistic and far-sighted attitude adopted by foreign personnel who came to lend a hand here. For that reason, Sister Lyn would have given a great deal for some graduates who were willing to stay on. It was hard to get good ones for future leadership, because they could make a better living almost anywhere else.

To add to the complications, accommodation for graduates in the student hostels was limited, and the only place for graduates to live in the crowded Rekso Road area was with relatives, if they had any. If they didn't have relatives obliged to find a corner for them somewhere, then there was no-where. So, they just moved out from the hospital to find work. It was a lot to ask young graduates to continue, mused Sister Lyn, when prospects were so limited.

But the work had to keep on developing. Surely there would be some who could stay. And surely, all those *sambutan* must be almost through ... so many people packed into this warm, stuffy room. Sister Lyn's head began to droop. She jerked it upright guiltily when, quite close to her, someone's chair grated. Dr. Hartono stood up and grasped the microphone. The welcomes and advisings were over. She hoped no one had noticed her impolite lapse. That was the worst of sitting up in the public eye.

"Young people, graduates," began Dr. Hartono, in his soft, clipped syllables. "You have qualified to serve your country and your people in a particular way. A vital part of this nation's development and modernization awaits you in the field of health. It is our hope that during your time here, you have not only learned to care for a patient's medical needs, but also to recognize the ultimate in healing — the needs of his spirit. May there be a wholeness in your future service wherever it is." The audience was alert again, all eyes on the speaker, sensing his earnestness.

"You will make mistakes," he continued, "as you have made them here. Be thankful that God does not expect perfection in all that we do in His name. But He does expect our best. The miracle of the loaves and fishes shows that God can do wonders with a very small offering. The medical care you offer, you may feel is small and inadequate, but, done in Jesus' name — will He not bless it?" Though quiet, his voice penetrated the whole hall, compelling attention. The medical superintendent had a way of getting across his ideals. A brief consultation with the head tutor followed. Then the medals were pinned on and the diplomas given out to forty delighted graduates.

"Chepto," a voice whispered — his own voice. "This is what you came for. You've got your education. Here it is, on this little scroll of paper, tied with a ribbon, and signed by Dr. Hartono." He ran his fingers up and down its smooth surface thoughtfully. He was back in Chimanuk, a school-boy who chose the long way home through the rice fields for privacy's sake, because he was eaten up with a longing for learning and training that could not be satisfied. It made him grin to himself to think of it, and of the value he had placed on this piece of paper. He said to the voice:

"It's not the diploma; it's what you do with it that matters. Your best ... the medical care you offer ... in Jesus' name ... thank you Bapak Doctor." As he pondered, the first part of the programme was giving way to the second — food and fun. There was a time for everything, he thought. Now it was time to celebrate, not meditate!

A *gamelan* had arrived, and its members were making a commotion as they set up their gongs and drums at the foot of the dais. The girls had changed from uniforms into the elegant ethnic costumes they had managed to acquire for the occasion — glowing brown and gold *sarung*, gay multicoloured blouses, sheer shimmering headscarves. "Enough to dazzle a fellow," thought Chepto, "so that he can scarcely recognize out-of-uniform classmates."

Some groups of students presented original tableaus that they had prepared in honour of the graduates; others had arranged special songs; and the Balinese students offered some of their exquisite dances, accompanied by the *gamelan*.

Outside, the guests were being served rice in little, bowl-shaped containers of folded banana leaf. A tangy, spicy smell that made the nose wrinkle and the mouth water hung over the table where the dishes of meat were laid out. Holding their basic serving of rice in one hand, the guests helped themselves from the meat table as they fancied with the other. Tinkling music blended with the chatter. Colour, movement, sound, smell — each contributed to the atmosphere of a magic occasion they would always remember.

A feast was the accepted way of celebrating any special event. The usual hostel fare was simple. Each mealtime everyone's plateful of rice and spoonful of vegetables lay dished and ready in the hostel dining area. Once or twice a week the menu varied when a couple of cubes of meat or beancake decorated each white mound. So for the hostel dwellers it was no celebration without a feast.

"Well, this may be my last opportunity." Chepto laid eyes on the meat table. Then he chuckled, efficiently tucking in to an enormous fish smothered in red sauce. Near him, the Sumatran girls were talking excitedly between mouthfuls.

"When are you taking off?" he asked them.

"Tomorrow. The money for our fares is here. Yes — sorry to leave you all so soon, but we have a promise to keep." They had been given a starting date for their first position in the hospital in North Sumatra. Chepto wondered if he would ever meet them again. It was so far away.

"Don't know when I will be going!" The boy from Kalimantan stopped talking to pull a cube of meat off a saté stick with his teeth. "Mail is so slow in Central Kalimantan. Do you know that it takes a week by boat up the river from the coast to get to our area — that is, when there is a boat. Over there they mightn't even know I am due to sit finals yet."

"And when are you leaving, Chepto?" The inevitable question was doing the rounds. Chepto, his mouth full of fish, finished munching.

"Mm! That tasted good. Oh, I will be moving on as soon as my plans mature."

The following day, many graduates were free for farewells and tidying up. When Chepto looked at the hostel mail rack he found a note there for himself. "Please report to the medical superintendent's office at eleven o'clock," he read. It wasn't far off that time now. So he sauntered away along the covered walk in the direction of the administration block, feeling mildly curious.

When he came out of the doctor's office he went straight back to the hostel. Rusdi met him on the way and called out, but Chepto passed him by, looking ahead. When Rusdi got no response he turned and followed, trying to analyze the odd expression he had noticed on his friend's face. "He went right by me and didn't even hear!" thought Rusdi. Aloud he called out: "Heh Chep, what's been happening? Don't tell me the army has rejected your application — a fellow as fit as you!"

"No, it's nothing to do with the army," Chepto slowed down his pace and turned to face his friend. His voice echoed surprise and unbelief. "I've been asked if I will stay!"

"You mean stay on here?" It was Rusdi's turn for surprise. "Bet you hadn't thought of that!"

"No one does!" Chepto wasn't keen to share this just yet. It was too new, and he hadn't fully grasped it himself. He felt dazed.

"Go on. What's the plan?" Rusdi pressed him.

"It's in the operating room. There are two of us they want to teach to be surgeon's assistants and to do anaesthetics."

"So ...?" Rusdi was a nuisance. And they were standing in the middle of the walkway where people passed by all the time with their ears cocked.

"So Bapak Doctor said think it over." Chepto stalked off. He wasn't prepared to talk any more; he wanted to be by himself. The hostel suddenly seemed more full of people than it ever had. He would have to go for a walk to be alone — out in the crowd.

He slipped through the hospital gate onto Rekso Road, past a line-up of pony-carts waiting to be hired; past the roadside barber who was clipping hair under a scruffy little tree. The barber recognized Chepto and called out, while his client looked at himself in a mirror hung on one of the branches. Chepto scowled back. Up and down Rekso Road the living stream of humanity flowed as usual. Chepto joined it.

"I wouldn't mind staying," he said to himself. "It's the work I like. But now that we are staff we can't go on living in the student hostel forever. And how is a fellow to exist when he has no family near to allow him a corner somewhere in their home? And the money? Everyone supplements their earnings with a secondary job, but how can operating room staff doing call duty manage that?" There was no way that he could see.

He imagined himself working a fiddle with drugs in order to run his own little practice on the quiet, as he knew some did — and dismissed the thought! It was the same old problem. Economic paralysis still gripped his country, and prevented ordinary men from getting ahead. Would it ever be different? Something told him it would, but he couldn't wait that long.

Chepto tramped on. From behind him a *becak* driver urgently sounded the clapper on his vehicle almost in Chepto's ear. He jumped onto the dust at the side of the road. Unaware of where his feet were taking him, he must have got too far out onto the highway. He resumed his theme, wrestling with himself.

"Everyone knows a graduate can't live without some kind of other job — even one who is single, that's clear enough! And as for one who plans to marry ...!" Then however could he afford the luxury of doing the work he liked? The whole thing was impossible!

He wished Lukas was still around. Lukas had a way of looking at a situation and getting it into a right perspective. He was strong on priorities. But Lukas had graduated the year before, and had gone to the school for evangelists "preparing to be a better minister to the whole man", he had said. And it was Chepto who had become senior student in his place. What a choice that had been, he thought! Here he was, in a tangle over his own decisions, let alone able to help anyone else with theirs.

It was Sri who would swing things one way or the other! They could marry — just as soon as he could find a job that paid enough, and some place to live. They would both continue working. Two could live as cheaply as one! But if he was to stay on at the hospital and learn special duties, he couldn't see how there would ever be a wedding. Well, at least he owed it to Sri to find out what she thought before scrapping the whole business and approaching the army. He had a right to get married, hadn't he?

Chepto swung around, retraced his steps along Rekso Road to the hospital gate, and went to look for Sri.

Outside the girls' hostel the flowers that Ibu Anna had planted were blooming, matched only by the rainbow-coloured cushions in the chairs on the verandah. Slivers of sunlight shone through the bamboo blinds, making a pattern on the furniture.

Chepto didn't have to wait long before Sri came

out onto the blind-shaded verandah. She was in uniform ready for afternoon duty, her long hair swept up under her little cap, and her figure slim and trim in her gleaming white cotton smock. Her skin was smooth, warm brown, like a ripe *sawo*,[2] and her black eyes glowed, radiating life and health. She was good to look at, and as he looked, Chepto wanted her.

At his news, her face lit up with pride. They didn't ask just anyone to stay. It was an honour.

"If it's right," she said simply, "you do it, and we will wait and see what happens."

Strange! She didn't have hangups about it like he did.

He wanted to say: "But Sri, don't you understand? Can't you see? This involves us! We can't get married if ..." But somehow, he couldn't. Instead, he found himself thinking: "She hasn't helped decide anything! She's only given me the freedom to make my own choice."

The next thoughts came pushing in almost unbidden, filling his mind and excluding all else. Choice — yes! Not chance any more, or fate! It was a matter of choice before God — the God who knows what is in each man's heart, and who cares about what He finds there.

For "it is He who has made us what we are, and given us new lives from Jesus, so that we may carry

---

[2] *Sawo* — a fruit with smooth brown skin. The classical description of a beautiful complexion, probably equivalent to the English "like a ripe peach."

out those things that He has planned for us"[3]. And Chepto knew deep down, that it would be choices like this all the way for the followers of Jesus.

Chepto stood there still looking at Sri, but seeing something else — a glimpse of "those things that God has planned". If God's work for him was to be here after all, then ... Wasn't his future in God's hands? Then he could choose what he believed God was showing him. He couldn't afford to choose anything else! He could trust God too, when it came to these other, more personal matters that were concerning him so. Sri was prepared to; she had hinted as much.

"You will know what His purpose for you is when the time comes." That was what Bapak Jonas had been trying to get across to him on the visit to Chimanuk. And the time was now. "If you truly want to honour God with all your heart," Jonas had said, "you will choose the right way." The choice that honours God. What you have and are ... in Jesus' name.

And Chepto knew he was going to stay.

---

[3] Ephesians 2:10 The Living Bible.

Epilogue

Chepto's story has really only begun. Its continuing chapters are being lived out in daily experience.

Since the years described here, a tide of change has swept through the Republic of islands; change that has meant development and growing economic prosperity; change that has brought to the humblest peasants in the remotest green atolls an awareness that they have a part in the work of national rebuilding.

At the hospital too, there has been change.

No longer can a candidate enter the School of Nursing as simply as Chepto did. New student hostels rise several floors above the old ones. For the likes of Chepto and Sri, married staff accommodation has become available among the mass of little homes with orange tiled roofs on the other side of Rekso Road. And there are other young graduates staying on and taking over responsibility as the old faces withdraw.

A young "Bapak" supervizes the boys' hostel. Ibu Anna has returned to America, and one of her former students faces with courage and resourcefulness the demanding task of mothering the "family" in the girls' hostel.

Another medical director sits at Dr. Hartono's desk, and where Dr. Daniel led his team, different surgeons work with more modern equipment. Foundations have been laid for a new operating suite. In fact, there are plans for an entirely new hospital growing up out of the old.

Change confronts these new leaders with continuous challenge; the challenge of presenting God's unchanging truth always in a contemporary setting; the challenge of living lives that demonstrate the love of Jesus, the Son of God, reaching out to people everywhere.

Did you enjoy reading this book? If so, here are some more you might like.

PEARL

"You must be in love, Tara!" laughed her brother. "I've heard them say that love is blind, but this is ... hey, wait a minute, there's no need to get upset. I'm only joking!"

Mutiara was standing rigid, her hands to her head and a look of dismay, almost of fear, in her eyes. "No ... no ... it's just that ... oh, what's *wrong* with me!"

TO A DIFFERENT DRUM

"Grabbing my sickle from the table, Mike began to run, heading for the gate. As soon as I realized what was happening I tore right after him — I wasn't going to have him kill his father with my sickle!"

What had brought Pauline Hamilton, a physiology Ph.D, to work with delinquent boys in Taiwan? Why had she chosen to march to a different drum from her contemporaries?

IN HIS TIME

Ian Gordon-Smith was killed in a road accident in Thailand, along with eleven other missionaries and children. Assured of a brilliant future, he had been willing to sacrifice it in order to be obedient to the Lord he loved. This moving story is told by his mother mainly through his diaries.

WHEN GOD GUIDES

Does God guide individuals? Is guidance confined to the big things of life, or can I refer everything to Him? In this book guidance is clothed in flesh and blood, as 27 people share their experiences in relation to marriage and children, houses and staff, missionary call and type of work, and the manifold details of everyday life.